P9-BJG-273

CONFIDENCE AT THE BOARD ROOM TABLE

Understanding and Managing Risk

HUGH GOLDIE

Copyright © 2007 by Hugh Goldie

All rights reserved. No part of this book may be reproduced in any manner whatsoever without written permission, except in the case of brief quotations embodied in critical articles and reviews.

Printed and bound in Canada by Art Bookbindery

www.artbookbindery.com

ISBN 978-0-9808992-0-7

Acknowledgements

Thanks to those who provided time, advice, and council in the development of the ideas presented in this book.

My wife Elaine who patiently listened as the ideas took shape on the beaches of Maui.

My colleagues at the Exchange Group, our CEO Peter Wintemute and the Honourable Gary Filmon, an Associate of the firm who helped me to sharpen those ideas.

Gord Holmes and Rennie Zegalski who read my manuscript and gave me the encouragement to continue and finish.

Mr. John Fraser whose broad experience as a CEO and Director redirected my thinking on several issues.

Dr. Paul MacAvoy, Educator, Corporate Director, and Scholar, Author with Ira Millstein of "The Recurrent Crisis in Corporate Governance." He read my first text on risk management and encouraged me to greater depths in analysis and approach.

My mentor and advisor Sheldon Bowles who, with Ken Blanchard, has written several best sellers for the business community including Raving Fans and Gung Ho. To him I owe special thanks. He tutored me on style, language, and presentation, and read several versions with the ultimate in patience.

CONTENTS

INTRODUCTION

Would you buy a house if the only way you could see what's inside was to look through the windows? That's literally what every Director is required to do.

Unlike the CEO and senior management, Directors aren't around day-to-day. They can't observe events as they unfold. Instead, they meet in the board room, six to eight times a year to attend Board meetings that last from two to ten hours, and review information prepared by the CEO.

Given that fleeting time frame and their reliance on the CEO, how can Directors fulfil their responsibility for monitoring and supervising the CEO? How can you be held accountable for the reputation and financial well being of the enterprise you serve, when you're only an outsider looking in? What windows do you look through to gather and assess the information you need to "buy the right house?" That's the challenge faced by all directors, from non- profits to major corporations.

To bridge the time and knowledge gap, effective Boards rely on their capabilities as risk managers. They specify the information they want to see through ten risk windows that give the board an almost compete view of the inside of the house. By examining the CEO's management through each risk window, the board can monitor and supervise the CEO, contribute to the CEO's decisions, and fulfill its mandate of preserving the reputation and financial well being of the enterprise.

Risk management is a key skill for Directors. Fortunately, it's a skill at which you're probably already proficient. You've been identifying and managing risk for most of your life. With experience you've learned to apply it to complex situations like buying a house, considering a promotion, or making an investment. You assess the risk, weigh your options, and consider the consequences. With each decision you become more skilled and confident in your ability.

This book is about taking your risk management skills to the next level and applying them with confidence at the boardroom table. Follow Mark Springfield as he presents his board with a plan that sorely challenges the Directors of his company and puts his job on the line.

MARK'S BLOCKBUSTER

Mark Springfield strode down the corridor, headed for the Eggs Inc. Boardroom.

The angry phone calls he'd received in the past week and the buzz emanating from the open boardroom door told him that he was in for some hot debate. "I can't say I blame them," he thought. "I said I would prepare a new plan for today's meeting but they never expected a radical change in direction. I suppose I should have kept them informed but I couldn't take a chance on a leak. I'll know by the end of the day if I've built a case that will bring enough of them onside."

Immediately that he stepped inside the Boardroom door an irate Ron Shendor yelled, "Mark, are you out of your mind? This enzyme stuff is nothing more than a pig in a poke and you're prepared to risk our whole company on it. You'll ruin us all"

INTRODUCTION TO EGGS INC

Mark is President and CEO of Eggs Inc. His grandfather Joseph immigrated to this country in 1920. When the clerk at the immigration desk took one look his long Polish name he decreed its English translation to be "Springfield." Grandpa Joseph didn't bat an eye. He took the name, and promptly did what he had learned from his father. He built a chicken coop and started a flock of laying hens. Soon he was in business, distributing fresh eggs to his new community. He always smiled and he was always there when he said he would be. He quickly became a favourite of his customers and the other egg producers in the area. When the local grocery chains tried to reduce their egg price by setting egg producers in the community against each another, Grandpa Joseph organized a producer's co-op that successfully fought the chains and retained producer's margins.

When Joseph's son William became the Co-Op President, he led its incorporation into Eggs Inc. In the late fifty's the company entered the market for powdered egg products, building a new plant in 1968. The company now processes eggs gathered from a 600-

mile radius, producing products for the food services industry.

The original seven families, now the sons and granddaughters of the founders, still own Eggs Inc. Each has a family member representing them on the Board. Only one Director, Frank Butler is an egg producer. All the others, except for Rachel Adams, are employed by other companies or the State government. Rachel is president of her own small company.

An opportunity disguised as a threat

Eight months ago, Mark was disturbed by a conversation with a buyer of a national bakery chain. The buyer, a close friend, confided that margins in the bakery business were declining and that his management was looking for ways to reduce costs. One proposal was to try a bidding system amongst suppliers that would force a reduction in raw material costs. Like other industries, they were trying to compel suppliers to be more competitive. Mark saw the move as a threat to Eggs Inc. His company's margins had also been declining. This move would reduce them even further.

"That's the problem with being in a commodity business," he thought," as he wrestled with how to respond. "Our long term heath and growth are at the mercy of the marketplace. How can we get away from that stranglehold."

His search for opportunities led him to the U of M's Poultry Department.

A research team in the department had developed a new process to extract high value enzymes from albumen (egg whites). The enzyme Lysozyme is a preservative used in the food industry. The enzyme Avidin is used in the biotech industry for immunization studies. These enzymes are in great demand, commanding $6000 per gram. The amount of enzyme in each egg is minute. Approximately 400 kilo's of albumen is required to produce one kilo of enzyme so a large supply of eggs is required.

Mark is proposing that Eggs Inc. take advantage of its large supply of eggs by investing in a plant to produce Avidin and Lysozyme. A prototype extraction process has been developed by the University but has not yet been scaled-up to production volumes. Mark is proposing a three-phase development project to scale-up and produce the product. The new plant will help to maintain Eggs Inc. margins and provide a new avenue of growth in a market with little competition. If they could get a head start with this new process they could become the world leaders in enzyme production from eggs and reduce their dependence on the commodity products going to the food services industry.

The estimated investment is $11.5 million over a four-year period. Mark sought out Ian Black of Equity partners Inc. to supply new capital in return for 25% of the company's shares and a seat on the board. The project is forecast to produce a 41.9% return on investment and create annual revenues for the company of $15 million within ten years, a 50% increase over current revenues. The university agreed to sell the rights to use the process for a 5% share in the company.

Mark recognized the risks inherent in such a development project. To manage the risk he hired the two university professors who developed the process to be on his development team. He is convinced their participation will virtually guarantee success. Mark also made an arrangement with Phasor-Heston, a pharmaceutical distribution company, to sell Avidin into the immunodiagnostics market, a market that Eggs Inc. does not know.

At today's meeting Mark is asking the Board to approve phase one of his plan and agree to the following steps.

1. Approve the plan in principle,

2. Approve the expenditure of $500,000 to proceed with phase one trials in conjunction with the University's Research Development Fund and to prepare the preliminary design for the phase-two pilot plant.

3. Agree to the sale of 25% of Eggs Inc shares to Equity Partners Inc for $7M.

4. Agree to the sale of 5% of Eggs Inc. to the University Research Development Fund.

5. Approve the expansion of the Board to nine members.

MARK PRESENTS HIS PROPOSAL

It took three hours for Mark and his team to explain the proposal, concluding with Jerry Surrey's presentation of the project financials. They showed a four-year negative cash flow as the new process facility was built and brought on stream, then a sweeping upturn in net earnings as sales of the new enzyme products took off. The internal rate of return came in at 41.9%.

When Jerry had finished presenting the financial statements, Mark rose. "Mr. Chairman that is my proposal. I move that the Board approve it as presented."

"Over my dead body," yelled Ron Shendor.

"Patience Ron," said the Bill Favro, the ever patient Board Chair. "You'll get your turn to comment. Will someone second the motion?"

Richard Butler raised his hand. "Seconded by Richard," responded Bill. "Now I think we should break for lunch and then open the debate when we return."

Ron Shendor jumped in. "Bill, if we are having the typical soup and sandwich lunch, I suggest we fill our plates and get back to the discussion. I think it will take us more time than Mark believes."

With the agreement of the others, the Chair declared a quick break, asking the presentation team to wait in an adjoining room in case there were questions.

"Mark doesn't get it," Ron Shendor said to Stan Koslowsky as they walked down the hall to the washroom. "He dropped this proposal on us with little notice and expects us to give him the go-ahead at this meeting? How could any of the Directors justify such a fast decision to their next family meeting? We'd all be roasted alive."

The body language isn't good Mark thought as he waited for this turn at the sandwich tray. It's a no win situation. Ron Shendor thinks my proposal is too risky. He sees it as a threat to his income and he's worried about his family's reaction. He has a lot of influence with the older members of the board. But they wouldn't be happy with the loss of income they'd suffer down the road if we didn't make some changes. I think I'm doing my job as CEO. I'm looking out for the future of this company. What else do they expect me to do?

WHAT SHOULD THE BOARD EXPECT FROM MARK?

Mark is the business leader, the CEO. CEO's are expected to manage the company with the best interests of the shareholders in mind, recognizing their appetite for risk. They are expected to assess the opportunities and threats in the market, develop strategies and plans to tackle them, and above all, to make money.

Under Mark's leadership, Eggs Inc has produced great returns for its shareholders. Mark believes his plan will continue the company's success. The plan took six months to develop with the help of his senior management team and several advisors. It tackles the market threats he has identified. It takes the company into a new and exciting production technology, and a very profitable line of products. While he is comfortable with its inherent risk, several of the Board Members are not.

The Board of Eggs Inc is accountable to the company's shareholders. Shareholders expect the Directors to provide regular assurance that their objectives are being met, and their investment is not in danger. To provide those assurances, the Board expects Mark to provide them with regular reports identifying his plans, his progress in achieving those plans, and the risks the company is facing.

When his reports suggest that objectives are being met and risk is within acceptable limits, the Board can relax a little. It will continue to monitor carefully but remain passive. When Mark's plans and reports suggest danger, the Board will typically heighten its activity and involvement. Mark's proposal has introduced a level of risk beyond the Directors expectations, and the Board has reacted as it should. It now must decide whether it is prepared to accept the risk on behalf of shareholders.

Identifying and Managing risk is a daily activity

We deal with risk daily. First we foresee that a risk could occur then we act to manage it. A risk is an event or situation that would stop or restrict us from reaching an objective. Risk has two dimensions, the likelihood of occurrence, and the impact if it does occur. It can never be eliminated but we can reduce the likelihood that a risk situation will occur, and we can reduce the impact if it does occur. Managing up front, avoids serious problems down the road.

One risk we manage every day is the possibility of a car accident. Foreseeing the possibility of risk is easy. We see evidence on the roadside and in the news every day. We reduce the likelihood of an accident by learning defensive driving skills, by following traffic rules, and driving sober. We reduce the possible impact of an accident by purchasing insurance, keeping our cars well maintained, and by using seatbelts and air bags. Our risk management strategy gives us confidence to drive to work in heavy traffic.

The Board's task is to decide if Mark's proposal is worth 'driving to work,' and whether it has enough 'seat belts and air bags' to make Directors comfortable with the risk.

Can Mark's team scale up the extraction process as planned? That's Mark's biggest risk. The viability of the project depends on meeting the targets for volume and cost of production he has established in his plan. The impact of failure would be significant. The investment in the project would be lost. Mark would lose credibility amongst his Directors. And his equity partner would demand a greater say in managing the business.

To reduce the likelihood of failure Mark has hired the two experts who developed the process. Professor Bill Sinclair of the University's Poultry Department knows the product. Professor Ernie Johnson of the Chemical Engineering Department knows the process. Working together, Mark believes they have a high probability of success.

To reduce the impact of failure, he will scale-up the process in three steps, reducing the capital at risk in each step.

Mark believes these risk-management strategies should avoid problems down the road, and satisfy the board's concerns and expectations.

WHAT SHOULD MARK EXPECT FROM THE BOARD?

While Mark is confident that his plan has a high probability of success, he expects the Board to contribute to its success. He expects them to apply their knowledge and experience to question, test, and enrich his assessment of the risks inherent in his strategy.

But how can a Board that meets only six times a year, be of any value to Mark or to the company? How can they provide the support that Mark should expect? How can they protect the best interests of company and its shareholders? While the directors know the egg business as it exists today, they are not actively engaged in the business. They know little about extracting enzymes from egg albumen. They are unfamiliar with the medical diagnostics market. They were not involved in the preparation of the plan and they've had less than a week to review it.

The Board contributes by acting as a mentor to Mark. It can't manage the business. It can help Mark to better view the risks inherent in the business and in the strategies he is proposing to manage the business. It performs like a mirror, using its knowledge and experience to reflect back to him, aspects of the plan that might be weak or flawed; aspects he cannot see, has not thought about, or is blind to because of lack of experience.

And it presents the reflection in a way Mark will accept as valuable. Only a CEO with courage can stand before such a mirror.

Conversely, a defective mirror cannot provide a true reflection. A board that lacks competence and credibility cannot be a credible support to Mark.

Not all CEO's share this view.

Some CEO's are antagonistic toward their Boards. They consider them to be a meddlesome and unnecessary impediment to their freedom. They see board questions and comments as a threat by uninformed pretenders. They withhold information from the Board and make significant strategic decisions without consulting the Board. The Directors are constantly struggling to stay informed.

Some CEO's don't know how to use their Boards, and often the Directors are equally unaware of how to help their CEOs. Some CEOs have created their Boards as statutory figureheads, tucked safely under their control. These are the 'yes" Boards, often composed of friends and advisors who are also paid for the non-board work they do for the corporation.

Some CEOs, however, recognize that Directors can bring strength and experience to their uphill battle for growth and success. They understand that a Board and CEO, working in complimentary roles, can be a tremendous force for boosting competitive advantage.

The Board is most effective when the Directors are respected by the CEO as welcome allies who bring complimentary knowledge, skills, and experience, and who provide a forum to test strategic ideas. CEOs with the confidence to lead, know that critical decisions are best made by good minds working together in what Jeffrey A. Sonnenfeld of Harvard University calls, "A virtuous cycle of respect, trust, and candour." [1].

Satchel Page, the baseball player sage, once said, "None of us is as smart as all of us." His comment applies to decisions of direction and strategy. It applies to those decisions relating to the management of a significant crisis. These kinds of decisions are rarely black and white with clear, simple, and predictable outcomes.

As we return to the board meeting we will learn how the Board deals with its uncertainty, and whether Mark has met the Directors expectations. Remember that Eggs Inc. and its Board differ from big listed public companies. The Eggs Inc. Directors are also shareholders with their own vested interests. Mark is the largest shareholder. The dynamics of the company and its Board are different from those of a large public company, but the role of the Board should be the same; to protect the best interests of the company and its shareholders.

---

[1] *What Makes Great Board Great, Harvard Business Review, by Jeffrey A. Sonnenfeld*

WHERE ARE YOU TAKING THIS COMPANY?

When the group settled with their lunch, Bill Favro re-convened the meeting, knowing he needed to reduce the tension. "Mark, your proposal sounds very attractive," he began. "Are there any questions from the group?" After the laughter subsided he continued, "If you all agree, I would like to organize the discussion by asking for clarification questions first, and then debating whether we want to support Mark's proposals."

Ron Shendor burst out, "Mark, you're idea is absolutely outrageous and …."

"Hold on Ron," said Bill Favro, interrupting Ron's attack. "You know my job as Chair is to ensure an orderly debate. I will acknowledge each speaker. Please address your questions to me. Since you started Ron, we may as well start with you."

"Mr. Chairman," said Ron, "Mark's proposal is attractive on paper, but I want to know why we need to go in such a radically different direction. We have a strong business we know like the back of our hand. Our annual growth has been a healthy 10%. Our margins are steady and we have no debt. We have a strong cash position, and we are paying regular dividends. This proposal aims to increase our growth and profitability, but at the cost of reducing some dividend payouts in the short-term, and with the assumption of a lot of risk. Is the return worth the risk? Why do we need to stray from our present course? Mark, what evidence do you have that the baking industry will threaten our margins? I've never heard of it. Our family does not accept this plan. Its too risky and we want it killed." Ron waited in silence, staring at Mark.

The Chair recognized Mark. "These are good questions Ron and I understand your concern for the risk this proposal brings to our operations. You are correct. Today we're doing fine, but we sell a commodity product. In the longer term I believe the market is becoming more competitive and our business risk will change. The emphasis our customers are placing on cost reduction is stronger than I have ever experienced. Competitive bidding systems are common for products that are of a commodity nature. I don't like the idea because it hides the benefits of a strong client-customer relationship. But we will be forced to deal with it."

"We also need to be constantly looking for ways to grow the business. The enzyme extraction process will give us significantly higher returns and enable us to retain the loyalty of our egg producers by paying them top dollar. I can visualize our plant attracting eggs from as far away as 1000 miles."

"Scaling up the extraction process is the big risk. We will do that in three steps to limit our capital at risk in the early phases. We will put measures in place to monitor costs, progress, and process performance, on a monthly basis so the Board will know quickly if we are succeeding or not. We are not familiar with the international marketplace for diagnostic materials. Using Phasor-Heston to distribute our Avidin product will mitigate that risk. Our fundamental strength is that we control a large egg supply. We need to keep our producers happy and we need to protect the supply of eggs for our traditional business. Is the reward worth the risk? That is what the board has to decide. However, the biggest risk we face is doing nothing and letting ourselves be squeezed out of business, if not by this threat, then by the next one to emerge."

Andrew Benson, the Board's only outside Director listened to Mark and thought, "This may be a good plan, but Mark hasn't told us what other alternatives he considered. Where is his assessment of the markets for Avidin and Lysozyme? Did he latch onto an idea he liked, and then make sure his plan supported it? And his presentation borders on confrontation. Perhaps that's the culture of this Board. Certainly Ron Shendor's question is more emotion than reason. Should I speak up? I don't have much history with this Board so I'll keep my ideas to myself for the moment. I wonder what questions the others will ask."

RISK WINDOW # 1 - DIRECTION, STRATEGY AND GOALS

Ron Shendor is not a big risk taker. He's frightened by Mark's change in direction into a business the company knows nothing about. The risks in the egg-products business are familiar and comfortable as are the competitors. The goals are clear, the strategies well understood, the, the revenues steady, and the dividends dependable. To him, the risk of more competitive bidding is business as usual, not a major risk to margins as Mark has claimed.

Ron represents his two younger brothers and his sister on the Eggs Inc. Board. Their dividends are an important top-up to their income, and they were upset when Ron showed them Mark's plan. They were tempted by the projected increase in dividend income, but balked at the significant risk that came with it. It didn't take long for them to conclude that Mark's initiative was an unnecessary threat to their lifestyles. They agreed that Ron should oppose it.

Ron and his family have good reason to be anxious. Mark's change of direction is fraught with many risks; new products, new competitors, new processes, new markets, new problems, inexperienced management, and unknown customers. Mark's new strategies are unproven; his new goals untested.

The Board must test Mark's reasoning, examine his assessment of the business risks, and assess his plans to manage them. The Board needs to be convinced that his plans accurately describe the company's business environment, its circumstances, and business risk. It needs to be convinced that his proposed change in corporate direction is both necessary and prudent, that his proposed initiatives are within the company's capabilities, and that his plan meets shareholder's appetite for risk.

The Board's knowledgeable and thorough examination of the plan is an important step in its validation. Good CEOs want to be sure that their own biases and interests are not a source of weaknesses that will cause their plan to fail in the marketplace.

Questions the Board Should Ask

The first questions a Director should ask when reviewing a strategic plan, or any other management proposal, concern direction, strategy, and goals.

1. Does this proposal change our direction or take us beyond our traditional mandate?

2. Does this proposal take us beyond our traditional level of risk?

Answering yes to either question should trigger additional questions:

Has Mark accurately assessed Eggs Inc. business risk? (Is the threat to Eggs Inc. margins as dire as Mark as has suggested?)

If the plan is successful, will the direction and strategy Mark has chosen mitigate the business risk?

Does Mark's plan demonstrate a knowledge and understanding of the risks inherent in its implementation?

Has Mark identified strategies to reduce or manage those risks?

Are there other viable alternatives less risky and more palatable than the chosen direction and strategy?

Are Mark's assumptions about the company capabilities reasonable?

Are Mark's assumptions about the reaction of competitors and potential customers, logical and prudent?

Are the rewards Mark has identified, worth the risks the shareholders are being asked to take?

Is the risk of doing nothing, worse than the risk of proceeding with this plan?

The final questions are the most important for the Directors.

Is Mark's plan likely to succeed? Can I accept the risk on behalf of the shareholders?

The Planning Process

These questions are part of the company's strategic planning process in which the Board and management together play important and complimentary roles. The planning process is an annual cycle. It includes the development of direction, strategy, and goals; the development of a business plan; the monitoring and assessment of results; and the development of changes required to fix or improve the plan. The CEO develops the strategic and business plans. The Board reviews and accepts them. The Board and CEO together monitor progress and report to the shareholders.

The intensity of the Board's involvement in the planning process changes with the level of risk in the plan, and with the confidence Directors have in the CEO. If Mark's plan had been simply to expand into a new market, the Board's need and desire to be involved would have been less intense. There would be competition and risk to consider, but those risks would be familiar, quantifiable, and more acceptable. Instead, Mark's plan takes Eggs Inc beyond its comfortable and familiar mandate, in a new direction, requiring a new and unproven technology, with unfamiliar risks. The Board must be more diligent in its review given the unknown nature of the risk, especially considering the surprising way it was introduced. And it must carefully consider its options.

The Board's Options

The Board is not in a position to construct a plan on its own. The Directors have neither the time nor the familiarity with the company's operating environment to do so. They must rely on Mark to present a plan for consideration; then they can ask the questions necessary to understand and assess it. The board can choose to accept Mark's plan as is, accept it with restrictions, ask for it to be reworked, or reject it. In extreme conditions, if the Board refuses to accept the risk and Mark refuses to change, it could ask Mark to resign, and hire a new CEO.

In our story, and in real life, CEOs can't prove their assumptions about the future. Nor can they prove that their plans will succeed. They can only ask the Board to review their plan, test their business judgement, make suggestions for change, rely on their track record of success, and accept the risk of doing so.

Key Points

In well run organizations with effective boards:

1. The Board does not construct a plan on its own. It relies on the CEO to present plans which it can accept as is, accept with restrictions, ask to be reworked, or reject.

2. The CEO relies on the Board's knowledgeable and thorough scrutiny of the plan to ensure that his own biases and interests have not created weaknesses that will cause it to fail in the marketplace.

3. The intensity of the Board's involvement changes with the degree of risk in the plan, and with the confidence they have in the CEO.

CAN WE FIND THE MANAGEMENT HORSES

"Rachel, you're next," said Bill Favro after Mark had concluded.

Rachel is the only Director who owns a successful business. Mark recognized her capabilities when, as an MBA student, she used Eggs Inc. as the basis for several school papers. When she wanted to buy a struggling high-end soft drink company after graduation, he gave her his support at the bank. With his help, she made it profitable and expanded its distribution to three other states. They meet regularly to exchange ideas and talk about their businesses. Mark thinks he learns as much from those meetings as she does.

"Mr. Chairman," Rachel began, "Mark's proposal acknowledges that our management team doesn't know the new process. What is left unsaid is how he intends to find people who do know the process. Have we identified managers and engineers who have done this type of development work before? What is the risk that we will hire people who don't know what they're doing and will fail to achieve our development timetable? I experienced this problem first hand and saw critical production problems go unresolved because the engineers we hired were not familiar with the process we hired them to manage. My company would have gone under had I not found an experienced production engineer to solve our problems."

"Mr. Chairman," said Mark as Bill Favro nodded in his direction, "The risk Rachel has identified is real, and the impact of failure could be high. But I believe our three-phased approach to development will successfully mitigate the risk. Most of the risk is in the first two development phases. It's in the development of the technology as we scale-up the process, and develop the process controls. Bill and Ernie will be leading the initial scale-up phases. As each phase proceeds we will be able to judge its success before we commit more time and money to the next. Once the scale-up has proven the technology and the process controls, the operations will become typical of any other processing plant."

"What assurance do we have that Bill Sinclair and Ernie Johnson will stay with us for the duration of the development phases," said Rachel? "And what experience do they have in scaling up a pilot plant?"

"The University," he replied, "has committed that Bill and Ernie will be seconded, part time to the project as part of the University's agreement. Their teaching load will be reduced. Scaling up our plant will be their research project and they'll be able to publish a significant research paper once the patents have been completed. We have not signed contracts with them. We should. They will be working part time but we have not concluded the details of their employment with us. That needs to be done."

"The answer to your second question is a real triumph for us," he continued, a broad smile breaking out on his face. "The University's Chemical Engineering Department recently lured Ernie Johnson away from the Research Department of Intercontinental Oil because of his reputation and experience with successful scale-up projects. Acquiring Ernie was a coup for the University, and attracting him to this project is a coup for us."

"Ernie and Bill will train our production staff during the two development phases. The budgets I presented included three new management positions, plant manager, plant engineer, and marketing specialist. Our plan is to assign managers from our present plant staff to these new positions. They will learn from Bill and Ernie during the scale-up phases. The individuals we have in mind are not scale-up specialists but they have proven their ability to manage our current operation. The changes will open opportunities, to promote several deserving supervisors in our existing plant."

"That is our plan Rachel. I believe we have covered the risk, except for some of the details relating to our relationship with the University and with Bill and Ernie. Those questions will be added to the list of questions that must be answered for the Board."

"Thank you," said Rachel smiling. "I am comfortable with your answer."

RISK WINDOW #2 - MANAGEMENT STRENGTH

Rachel is not questioning the quality of Mark's management team. She knows them well. She has watched Mark build their strength, and she believes they are competent. Her question asks whether Mark's strategy for filling management positions adequately addresses the risk inherent in a new processing operation with untried technology. Rachel's been there. Her experience adds to the board's competence and to the discussion. Her questions illustrate one facet of the risks inherent in Mark's development of his management team.

The management team is not necessarily a stable platform, particularly for growing companies that are adding new executives. Individuals can become disenchanted and seek other growth opportunities. Some need to be moved because they are unable to handle their growing responsibilities.

Next to the CEO, senior management is critical to directing the company's operations and achieving its goals. Team strength is demonstrated by four important attributes.

Competence: Individual team members are skilled in their specialties, and instil confidence in other team members and the Board that they can manage their portfolio under pressure.

Loyalty and Dedication: Individual team members are loyal to the company and dedicated to the achievement of its goals. They may not always like the situations they must manage, but they support the company's mission.

Capacity for growth: As the company grows the senior management team can manage the increased levels of risk and complexity that accompany growth. Capacity for delegation to others, particularly by the CEO/Owner, is an important attribute for growing companies.

Teamwork Team members work together and support one another's activities. The work of individual specialties is closely entwined. Each department depends on the others for their success, and for the success of the entire company.

Assessing Management-Team Risk

While the Board doesn't choose the executive team, the strength of the team is clearly an important risk factor for the board to monitor. It can assess and monitor Management-Team Risk in three ways.

The first is the observation of management performance by Directors at Board and committee meetings, or at informal gatherings. Directors continually observe the handling of issues at Board meetings and form opinions about how effectively they are managed. Some opinions are voiced as part of the Board's discussion, but many are not because the situation is not appropriate to make a comment, or because there is no appropriate forum to raise the issue. Withholding critical observations can make a bad situation worse. For example, incompetent management can be left in place long after Directors know there is a problem, simply because the opportunity to discuss the issue openly and candidly never arises. Director's observations are an important but poorly used risk management tool that receives special comment later in this chapter.

The second way the board can monitor Management-Team Risk is using a regularly scheduled review of the CEO's annual succession plan for senior management. As part of its risk management mandate, the Board should ensure that a successor to the CEO has been identified and is being groomed. It is also important that the CEO is identifying and grooming successors for his management team. For a growing company, the importance of a succession plan for the CEO and senior management cannot be overstated. Succession may not always be internal, particularly for fast growing companies.

During this review, the CEO should provide his assessment of the team's strengths and weaknesses, the risks inherent in individual team members, and his plan to manage those risks.

Sharing this information with experienced advisors, can assist the CEO to handle problem situations, and can help to avoid nasty surprises for the Board. On one occasion, a competent CFO left a company to the surprise of the Board. They were counting on the expertise and contribution of the departing executive and unaware of the growing rift between him and the CEO.

On another occasion the CEO became aware of weakness in a team member only through the observation of Directors. It's easy to be blinded to management ineffectiveness by personal friendship, by a sense of loyalty, or by being too close to an individual.

A third tool is a routine evaluation of the CEO's capacity to manage into the future. As companies grow and become more complex, every CEO approaches the upper limit of their capacity to lead and control in a larger more complex environment. Identifying CEO limitations isn't only a heads-up of an impending need for a replacement. It may be a heads up that the CEO may need additions to the management team. Unless of course the CEO refuses to acknowledge their limitation, then this weakness is a heads up of a serious problem. The Board should recognize the problem and acting to avert consequences down the road.

Director's observations

Earlier in this chapter we suggested that Director's observations are an important but poorly used risk management tool, primarily because there was no appropriate forum to raise issues openly and candidly. In one situation a director was struggling with the performance of what he perceived to be a seriously weakened CEO. Finally he raised his observations at an informal gathering of Directors following a regular Board meeting. To his surprise every director echoed his sense of frustration, and confirmed that their observations had been made over the past year. They also confirmed that they had been reluctant to raise the issue because of the implications of a turnover in leadership, and because they were not sure that the other directors would agree with their views. The CEO was replaced. Now, following each Board meeting, the independent directors hold an in-camera session to air, and sometimes record, Director's observations. The in-camera meeting is gaining in use with both for-profit and not-for-profit boards.

In our story, Rachel's question demonstrates how the Board can add value to the discussion and to the CEO's thinking. Her experience with a similar production problem has helped Mark to see weaknesses in his staffing plan. Her question is not a criticism of Mark but rather a supporting observation that will make Mark's plan better.

Key points

1. Next to the CEO, senior management is critical to directing the company's operations and achieving its goals.

2. Management team strength is demonstrated by competence, loyalty, capacity for growth, and teamwork.

3. Boards assess management strength using Directors observations, regular reviews of the CEO's succession plan, and by a routine review of the CEO's capacity to mange into the future.

ARE WE INCURRING UNNECESSARY FINANCIAL RISK?

Andrew Benson was next to be acknowledged by the Chair. Andrew is a Senior Analyst with Horizon Mutual Fund Company. The companies he deals with at Horizon are all large, sophisticated, and publicly traded. In comparison, Eggs Inc is small and unsophisticated. He finds the differences in sophistication a challenge.

Andrew is not sure how to judge Mark's plan. He could tear apart Mark's financial forecast as being incomplete and optimistic, without sufficient evidence to backup its claims. But perhaps his expectations would be overly sophisticated for this situation. Despite the lack of details, he does have a good feeling about this plan, and his gut tells him it could work.

As he reviewed the plan prior to the Board meeting, he concluded that Mark's failure to show the downside risk was an obvious and critical omission that required comment.

"Mr. Chairman, I am an outsider here and I am not as intimately familiar with the history of Eggs Inc as the rest of you. I would like a better understanding of how Mark's proposal could affect the financial strength of the company. Eggs Inc. is at risk for the seventy-five percent of the downside impact if the initiative should fail. Mark, have you calculated what the impact on our balance sheet would be if the project did fail at any one of the three phases you have outlined? Have you considered setting up a separate company for this venture? Could Eggs be one of the investors, along with Equity Partners Inc, plus others who think this is a great idea and are willing to take a risk? The additional capital could be raised privately or through an IPO. Eggs Inc. would not own as large a share but could still retain controlling interest."

"An interesting idea," said Bill Favro. "What do you think of it Mark?"

Mark was prepared for the question but it wasn't one he wanted to hear. If Andrew's idea were to gain favour with the Board it would weaken his family's control. Mark's Grandfather had established the family's control when he brought the local egg producers together as a cooperative in 1928. He became the undisputed leader with his successful fight against the grocery chains and their attempts to reduce prices.

When Mark's father John incorporated Eggs Inc. and took over the cooperative's business, he made sure that the Springfield family gained controlling interest. They were the largest producer by far. They acquired 35% of the shares based on their production volumes and the Springfield family's leadership. The other families received a ten percent interest except for Bill Favro's family which had fifteen percent. When critical issues came to the Board, the family was always able to muster enough votes to carry their ideas.

When Mark took over as CEO, his primary strategy was to bring more producers into the supplier group, but without any shareholder interest. They benefited as members of the group because they received higher prices than competitors were prepared to pay. Mark made sure that membership in the club was limited and was seen as a privilege.

Mark's strategy was to have Eggs Inc. as the main investor so he and his family would not have to put up any family money but would still retain controlling interest in a larger and more profitable company. If the new venture were set up as a separate company as Andrew was suggesting, then Mark's family would have to directly invest in order to retain control.

"Good questions Mr. Chair," Mark said. "No, we have not calculated what the impact of failure would be on our balance sheet. As to Andrew's second question, we have briefly examined the idea of a separate company but I am not sure that we would have the support of the bank if Eggs were not the primary owner."

"That means you are counting on the history and financial strength of Eggs Inc balance sheet to convince lenders to participate in the debt requirements of the new facility," said Andrew?

"Yes," said Mark.

"Then I believe we should know the downside risk," said Andrew. "We should see the numbers."

"Mr. Chair, we will do the calculations," said Mark, hoping the question of a separate company had passed.

RISK WINDOW #3 - FINANCIAL STRENGTH

Financial strength is a measure of the reliability of a company's cash flow, its ability to cover current liabilities, and its long-term debt. A financially strong company has many advantages over weaker competitors. It has ready access to capital at relatively low cost. It has the financial resources to take advantage of market opportunities. It can fund the research and development required to create new products, enter new markets, and keep ahead of its competition. A financially strong company can pay its bills and maintain strong relationships with its suppliers. It has greater freedom to make economic decisions and to weather economic downturns. It is less likely to default on its commitments to customers. In some cases, customers are willing to pay a premium to deal with a company they can count on.

Andrew's question goes to the core of the board's responsibility to protect the reputation and financial well-being of the company. What is the likelihood of failure? How much could we lose? What could be the impact on profits or dividend payments? How would relations with our bankers be affected?

While Mark is aware of the financial risk inherent in his plan, he knows that project failure is only one of the hazards that can affect financial strength. Marketplace initiatives by customers or competitors can reduce revenues and margins. Changes in interest rates, inflationary trends, changes in currency values, and looming periods of recession can compound the effects of project failure. They are issues that the CEO and Board should consider when planning a new project, or assessing the continuation of current operations.

The importance of quantifying downside risk is particularly critical for companies that are financially weak. Most important is a company's ability to service its current debt, and the current portion of its long-term debt. For Eggs Inc, debt is not a significant issue but for those companies with large outstanding debt balances, failure to generate the necessary cash flow could push the company into financial jeopardy, putting lenders in a position to dictate how the company will operate.

Eggs Inc. balance sheet and income statement show that the company is financially strong. It has a significant cash position. It has a history of successful growth and profitability. But how can the Board assess changes in financial risk? How far is too far, when new initiatives add debt, or impact free cash flow?

Boards use three tools to manage risk to financial strength.

The first is developing a policy that sets limits on critical ratios such as current ratio, total liability to total net worth, or debt service coverage ratio. These ratios are indicators of financial strength. Setting limits establishes benchmarks that provide direction to the

CEO for planning purposes or for routine monitoring. They are used by lenders to monitor risk to their investments.

The second tool is the quarterly monitoring of financial results. Highlighting ratios keeps the targets and the actual results in the Board's purview.

The third tool is the external audit. The Auditor provides an opinion on the accuracy of management's financial statements. They are the source of the data reporting financial strength. For both the Board and management, the accuracy and timeliness of the financial statements are critical risk elements.

Since the introduction of the Sarbanes-Oxley act in the United States and the subsequent changes to accounting rules in many other jurisdictions, more attention is being paid to the preparation of financial statements,

Andrew's hesitation

As a new and inexperienced Director, Andrew is reluctant to be forthright in his comments. It's a natural reaction. He doesn't want to look foolish by making an inappropriate comment. His strategy is ill advised. The strength of every Director is important to the board's ability.

Approaching board discussion from a risk perspective helps to reduce the anxiety of asking questions. Introducing a topic with the question, "Is this a risk issue that the board should be concerned with," will give the board an opportunity to consider it. Most boards would prefer new members to ask questions and learn, rather than keep silent. There are no dumb questions.

Key points

1. Financial strength is a measure of the reliability of a company's cash flow, its ability to cover current liabilities, and its ability to cover long-term debt.

2. Boards manage financial strength risk by establishing limits on critical ratios, and monitoring financial statements to track them.

DO WE HAVE THE SYSTEMS?

Frank James, Chairman of the Audit Committee, was next to speak. Frank is a retired egg producer who takes his role as Director seriously. He has no formal training in finance, or accounting, but over the years he has spent enough time with the company's auditors to learn what questions to ask at a Board meeting. Lately he's begun to feel that many of the issues confronting the audit committee exceed his understanding, but he's been reluctant to acknowledge his fears. He is unsure of who on the Board could replace him. In reviewing Mark's plan however, he made the link to a recent audit report and recognized the limitations inherent in the company's current financial systems.

"For the past two years our external auditor has commented that we are increasingly at risk because our financial system is insufficient to manage the growing volume and complexity of our transactions, or to provide critical financial and operating information on a timely basis. The Auditor has also been critical of our weakened financial controls. It seems to me that this proposal takes us into a new industry, significantly increases the size of the company, and adds immensely to that systems risk. Does this proposal address the systems issue?"

"Yes it does," said Mark. "Our current system has grown up with us and I acknowledge it is a nightmare. Our plan includes a new SpanMaster Enterprise Resource Planning (ERP) system that will provide better information, faster and at less cost. It will mean less duplication of effort and fewer people. It will allow for considerable expansion of our operations with little additional expenditure. The cost of the new system has been included in the estimates."

"Have you spoken to any users of the SpanMaster system?" asked Andrew, stimulated by the question and forgetting to address the Chair.

"Good question," said Bill Favro, interrupting Mark's answer. "Andrew, could you hold your question until Frank is finished? Frank, did you have a follow-up question?"

"Why do we have to bother with all this addressing the chair and being recognized by the Chair," said Ron Shendor. "It's a waste of time and this is serious business."

"It is serious," said Bill, "and it's also contentious. Ron, I think you will agree that when this Board has differences of opinion the discussion can get out of hand. Following Roberts Rules keeps the discussion on point, and at a calm and objective level."

"Frank, you have the floor," he continued.

"I think Andrew is better qualified to ask the follow-up," said Frank. "I know he has the experience. I understand the problem but I am unfamiliar with the solutions."

"In that case," continued Bill as he nodded to Mark, "We'll go ahead with Andrew's question."

"We have not spoken to any users," said Mark. "We have talked to the SpanMaster Sales Rep. to obtain sufficient information for this proposal. We also talked to the reps for several other systems. Our choice of SpanMaster was made on the advice of our Vice-President of Information Technology. He says it's the best one on the market for companies our size."

Andrew continued. "In my job as a Horizon Analyist, I've observed the results of many similar ERP installations. The scenarios are all the same. The system ends up costing was twice what supplier quoted, and takes twice as long to implement as the supplier projected. The disruptions to a company's operations are significant. Some thought they could take shortcuts from the supplier's recommended implementation procedure and they paid dearly for that mistake. They also found that the basic system the supplier proposed did not include important modules that were needed as their business changed."

"The implementation of the new system will be a real wake-up call for you. You will probably find that system documentation is not current and that many of your accounting and management personnel are not aware of the controls and procedures that are supposed to be in place."

"I have also learned that the so-called best system is not always the right one for a particular situation. In my experience IT people may not always be the best decision makers. They go for bells and whistles that are not are not always necessary or appropriate. Should you be consulting with other ERP users and get an idea of their experience? Have you considered speaking to an outside consultant? Is the head of your IT department sufficiently qualified to make this judgement? You may wish to revise your installation estimates and carefully examine other alternatives. Looking at your estimates, the ERP system is a significant part of your capital expenditure?"

"It is a large cost," replied Mark, "and from what you are saying the risk of cost runaway is also significant."

"Yes," replied Andrew, "but from what I have heard today, this company should be installing a new system whether you go with this proposal or not. Perhaps you could start now, recognizing that while adding the new plant will influence the specifications down the road, at least you will have a head start on solving some of the problems"

"We will rethink our approach to the ERP system. Good points Andrew," said Mark.

"Yes they are good points," Andrew thought to himself. "Mark, you have no concept of the difficulties you will encounter installing your new ERP system. Add that risk to the risks of new technology, new plant, and new market, and your capabilities as CEO will be taxed to the limits. One thing I am unsure of is the capabilities of the IT Vice-President. Does he have the capacity to pull it off, or will we be required to add new people?

Well, I've raised the point. I'll have to monitor his reaction over the next few Board meetings."

(Note: This is an example of why the Board should know the capacity of senior management team members.)

RISK WINDOW #4 - FINANCIAL SYSTEMS AND CONTROLS

Frank's point is a key to success for growing companies. Financial systems track the flow of revenues and expenditures. Financial systems provide data on profitability, cash flow, cost of quality, inventory levels, and working capital employed. These are a few of the important benchmarks the Board and management will use to track the company's performance and monitor the progress of Mark's development plan.

Controls establish procedures for managing and recording transactions, and for handling assets. They are essential to assuring the accuracy of financial information. They are instrumental in minimizing theft and fraud. Simple controls like requiring two authorizing signatures on all cheques, and separating responsibilities for ordering, receiving, and paying for materials, will reduce the opportunity for error or fraud.

Effective systems, with effective controls, allow management to create financial-and-management information that is timely, complete, accurate, and readily available. They allow for fast, effective planning and operating decisions, and for accurate and timely financial statements. Management are more able to manage risk, monitor performance, and be confident of their decisions.

The Board, to manage systems and controls risk, should ask two questions:

- Has management demonstrated that adequate financial systems and controls are in place and documented?

- Has management demonstrated that the policies and procedures, on which the systems are built, are being followed?

To answer these questions the Board uses three risk management tools. These are:

1. Management's presentation of system and policy documentation

2. The internal audit function

3. The annual external audit.

The way in which these tools should be used is well defined. The Board should seek assurance from the CEO that financial system documentation is in place, current, and being followed by all staff and management. Based on an audit plan approved by the Board, the internal auditor should review system documentation for adequacy, and then test the operation of internal systems and controls, assessing them for adequacy and compliance. The External Auditor, in assessing the quality of management's annual financial statements should use the internal auditor's review of system documentation and compliance, as part of their opinion. The Board's Audit Committee should approve systems and policy documentation, direct the activities of the external and internal auditor, and review their reports.

That's what should happen. The reality is often very different. The issue is of particular importance for private small and medium sized enterprises, (SMEs.)

From the Board's perspective, the risk to effective financial systems and controls has two main sources. The first is rapid growth. It's a problem for small companies like Eggs Inc, as well as for large multi-nationals. As companies grow financial systems become strained. When a low priority is assigned to system improvement, system documentation deteriorates and adherence to controls becomes more lax. The accuracy, reliability, and timeliness of financial information declines, inhibiting the Board's task of monitoring financial condition and progress against plan.

The second source of risk is systemic. The introduction of sophisticated computer systems had led to the belief that the controls were built-in. Management, in their efforts to trim costs, had reduced the resources available keep system documentation and system audit current. The recent focus on improved systems and controls resulting from the scandals of Enron and WorldCom has changed that attitude significantly.

Few SMEs and not-for-profit organizations have an internal audit function and many of their Directors are under the misconception that the external auditors will examine internal controls. This is not the case. In the absence of documentation describing the systems and controls, the external auditor will perform only a conformance audit, verifying the accuracy of stated assets and liabilities. With a conformance audit, financial controls are not evaluated thus weaknesses remain undetected.

To counter this risk, the function of the audit committee has been greatly enhanced in both effort and importance.

Key Points

1. Financial systems track the flow of revenues and expenditures through the company's books, providing data on profitability, cash flow, cost of quality, inventory levels, and working capital employed.

2. Controls establish procedures for managing and recording transactions, and for handling assets. They are essential to assuring the accuracy of financial information, and they are instrumental in minimizing theft and fraud.

3. To manage system and control risk the Board uses three risk management tools; management's presentation of system and policy documentation, the internal audit function, and the annual external audit.

WILL OUR FOOD SERVICES BUSINESS SUFFER?

Ron Shendor looked agitated. He sat on the edge of his seat, hunched over the table, red faced, like he was ready to pounce. "Do you have an urgent question," said Bill Favro. He was used to Ron's sudden and urgent questions.

"What about our regular business?" Ron asked. "Your plan doesn't even mention the business that keeps us alive and pays our dividends. It only shows up in the financial statements to support your great project. This proposal will divert the management's attention away from distributing egg products, and into a high-risk development project that has only been demonstrated in a laboratory. It could threaten Eggs Inc. stability and profitability."

"Mark, go ahead," said Bill.

"Good question Ron," said Mark. "I should have commented on that issue. As I mentioned in answering Rachel's question about staffing, we have strong and experienced management and employees. I have no concerns about our General Manager being able to handle our routine production. He handles it now. If anything, this new project will inject a little excitement into our management team as they receive promotions and take on new responsibilities."

"As for me, I will not be directly engaged in the new project. In phase one the work will be going on in the lab. When it moves over here, the personnel assigned to the project will do the work. I have said I will examine Rachel's concerns for staffing, but I believe the risk is low that our food service operations will suffer."

Good luck, thought Rachel as she listened to Mark's answer. This project will have its glitches like every other project and you will be drawn into the solutions. It's a good thing that your management team is as competent as you say.

RISK WINDOW # 5 – SECURITY AND USE OF ASSETS

Ron's point addresses a significant issue for SMEs, particularly those run by entrepreneurs who thrive on finding new and exciting challenges. For some, the thrill is in the discovery, the creation of a new idea and a new product. When a new and exciting idea comes into view they can easily forget the core business that made them successful.

For one-owner companies, the risk of such a diversion rests with the CEO/Owner. He or she can do what they want with their money. For growing companies with multiple investors, or for not-for-profit organizations, that risk has wider implications.

The shareholders expect Mark to expand the company, and increase revenues. But they also expect him to manage all of the corporation's physical, monetary, and human assets; equipment, space, people, intellectual property, and cash. They expect all the assets to be protected. They expect all the assets to be productive. Unproductive assets tie-up capital that could be used to generate profits or to pay dividends.

The Board should ensure that Mark is addressing potential risk situations related to the corporation's assets. Those risks include:

- Underused or unproductive physical assets such as poor space utilization or idle machinery.

- Staff or management personnel whose full productive capacity is unused. Using lean manufacturing principles to improve the layout on a factory floor can significantly improve both space utilization and cost controls.

- Theft of physical assets such as parts from inventory, medical devices from a hospital, or materials from a construction site.

- Working capital tied up in raw material inventories; work in process, finished goods inventory, or receivables.

The Board relies on the reports of the internal auditors to confirm that management has appropriate systems and controls in place to manage the security and use of the corporation's assets.

Key Points

1. Shareholders expect the CEO to protect and make effective use of all of the corporation's physical, monetary, and human assets; equipment, space, people, intellectual property, and cash.

2. The Board relies on the reports of the internal auditors to confirm that management has appropriate systems and controls in place to manage and protect the corporation's assets.

56

WILL WE HAVE TO DEAL WITH A NEW SET OF REGULATORS?

Rachel Adams had another question and was recognized by the Chair.

"Mark, the more I learn about this plan the more I am intrigued with its prospects. It sets us off in a new direction with a new challenge, and I like the idea of climbing the next mountain. I think this company is a strong as it is because we have not been afraid of challenge or change."

"Harrumph," snorted Ron Shendor. "How many times have we almost fallen off the mountain?"

Rachel continued unfazed. "One issue you have not raised is the possibility of change to our regulatory obligations. The egg business is heavily regulated today. Will we require approvals from a different regulator for this new venture?"

Mark responded to Bill Favro's nod. "Rachel, you're right, we have neglected to speak to the issue. We have researched our approval requirements, and yes, we will require approval for our new process and our new products. The regulatory authority is the same as we deal with now. Their personnel are familiar to us. We are highly regarded by them for our process quality and compliance. We will not be tasked with building new relationships. Proving our process and obtaining regulatory approvals will take time and is one of the reasons that our development project will take three years. It's also a reason for the high security. We want to commercialize the process as quickly as possible and in secrecy. At this stage we know the process works in a lab environment. To make it commercially viable, we need to improve the yield. We want to make the improvements and patent the improved process. As noted in the Board package I sent to you, the University is willing to sell the patent rights to us for use in the food services industry, in exchange for shares, and their right to use the new technology in non-competitive applications. We have completed a draft agreement with them on that issue. It also includes a requirement that we conduct the first stage of prototype development at our expense, at the University's SmartPark facility."

"Is the SmartPark a secure facility?" asked Rachel.

"Yes," said Mark, "but we will add our own security system as well."

"Are you saying The University will have the rights to use the extraction process we commercialize in other non-competitive situations?" asked Andrew.

"Yes," said Mark. "The process appears to have prospects for use in the oil industry."

"What is the risk that some large company with interests in both the oil and food services industries, could obtain and use the process through the back door?" responded Andrew.

At this point Bill Favro jumped in. "We're a long way from Rachel's question about regulatory issues. Mark, will the answer to Andrew's question take us down a new path of questions?"

"No," said Mark, "Because I don't know the answer to his question. I'm glad Andrew thought of this. I sure haven't, and I don't think our lawyers have either. We will examine the issue and report back to the Board."

"Rachel," said Bill, "Are you satisfied with Mark's answer to your original question?"

"Yes," said Rachel.

"Then let's move on," said Bill.

RISK WINDOW #6 - REGULATORY ISSUES

Mark and his management team are responsible for complying with a myriad of regulations. Directors can become personally liable for some obligations if the company fails or has not been compliant. The Board manages this risk by ensuring that management has identified and is complying with regulatory requirements.

Regulatory requirements originate from State and Federal Corporations Acts, securities regulators, taxation authorities, environmental authorities, health protection authorities, workplace health and safety acts, and labour legislation to name a few.

Corporations are required to file annual returns stating they are still in business and identifying current Directors and Officers. Failure to file could mean the company is operating illegally.

Taxation authorities require monthly reporting of employee source deductions for tax and state benefits, and the annual issuance of employee deduction summaries. As well, companies are obligated to file annual tax returns declaring revenues, expenses and taxable income, and to pay taxes owing.

60

Securities Regulators establish requirements for companies that are publicly listed. These requirements include rules for trading of securities, publishing of annual reports, timely and accurate disclosure of material events that affect the company's operations, and declaration of insider trading activities.

Environmental Protection Acts establish regulations defining allowable emissions of harmful vapours or liquids, and fines for failure to comply. Companies are usually not obligated to file routine reports indicating compliance. They are required to report incidents, and are subject to fines if they fail to do so.

Workplace health and safety legislation establishes regulations defining allowable safe work principles and practices. As with environmental legislation, companies are usually not usually obligated to file routine reports indicating compliance. They may be required to file notices of significant construction or excavation activities, and are usually required to report incidents or accidents. They are subject to fines if they don't. In some jurisdictions, Directors can be criminally liable if a company's fails to take effective safety precautions.

Companies in the food or healthcare products business must comply with regulations relating to process and product safety. Inspectors are often resident in the plant to ensure compliance. In many cases the regulator must approve processes, products, and plant layouts, before product may be produced for sale. The penalties for non-compliance can include fines or loss of a licence.

The Board's approach to managing regulatory risk is to solicit evidence from management that regulations, to which the company is subject, have been identified, and are being appropriately honoured. Many Boards ask for a signed management statement, presented at each Board meeting, stating that the necessary regulatory requirements for the period have been met. The internal and external audit functions also provide evidence of compliance.

Regulations Dictating Compliance by the Board

Some regulations, particularly those of securities regulators, recommend or dictate some governance practices for public companies. Complying with these regulations is the responsibility of the Board. While these do not necessarily apply to private, unlisted companies, it seems likely there will be a trickle-down effect over time.

Key Points

1. The CEO is responsible for complying with government regulations

2. Individual Directors can be liable if the company fails or has not been compliant with some regulations.

3. The Board manages this risk by ensuring that management has identified and is complying with regulatory requirements.

HOW DO WE KNOW THAT YOU WILL BE OPEN WITH US IN THE FUTURE?

Stan Koslowski was recognized to speak. Mark knew that his questions would not be easy. Stan's grandfather and Mark's Grandpa Joseph had been antagonists in the beginning, and their families remained so today.

"How do we know you are being honest with us today, and how do we know that you will be open with us in the future?" Stan said. "You obviously like the new direction you are trying to push us towards and you want to maintain the control that your family has exercised from the beginning. It seems to me that this proposal is geared to sweet-talking enough of us to go along so it will pass and your family can retain control. That's exactly what your father did when Eggs Inc was created."

Mark tried to hide his feelings about the long-term disagreements between families but his short sigh must have given them away. Stan's questions were rarely about fact and mostly about control and emotion. Mark found them hard to answer but he knew he had to show restraint. Besides, there was some truth in Stan's comments.

When the original cooperative became a corporation, some members, led by Stan's Grandfather, thought the shares should have been distributed evenly amongst the member families in the spirit of a true co-operative. Mark's family produced the most eggs for the co-operative and wanted the shares distributed according to production volume. They won the day, but not without creating some resentment that surfaced on occasions such as this one.

"Stan, you are welcome to go through any of the materials that form the background to this presentation. I admit that I have not been open with the board prior to today's meeting. That was because of the confidential nature of the negotiations with the University and our potential equity partner. I assure you that from now on I will keep this Board informed and report progress at each Board meeting. You will know what is happening."

"What about the control issue," Stan said? "Your family will still control the company in its new form. Inevitably some of us will go along so you will still hold enough votes to force the proposal down the throats of the rest of us. You can simply go ahead and do anything you want."

Bill Favro nodded towards Mark.

"Each Director is free to vote their shares in any way they want," responded Mark. "It's up to me to demonstrate the viability of this proposal. The history of this Board has been to find consensus and work from there. That's what I am looking for today. I believe the health of our company is threatened if we do not find some means of increasing the value of the products we sell. This proposal gives us pricing power. It won't increase the returns we receive from our powdered and liquid egg products, but it can increase our revenue by extracting and selling high-value enzymes from the raw material supply that we already control. It will allow us to pay our producers a premium over our competition and maintain our egg supply. We are changing direction slightly, but the change is consistent with our present business."

"What proof do you have that we are under threat?" yelled back Stan. "You're just trying to ram this proposal through!"

At that point Bill Favro jumped in. "Thank you Stan. You asked your question and made your point. You will have another opportunity to debate the issue when all our clarification questions have been answered. Can we move on?"

"Harrumph," said Stan, but he sat back in his chair and looked around the table for any sign of support.

RISK WINDOW #7 – COMMUNICATION

Stan Koslowsky may have an ongoing family feud with Mark but he also made a good point. The Board needs to know if it can trust Mark to be open with them in the future. The Board relies on Mark to be forthcoming with the information it requires to do its job of risk analysis. It has no other reliable source.

Secrecy breeds suspicion and distrust. It damages relationships. Communication is the lubricant of good relationships. It builds trust, loyalty, and good will. With positive good will, even the impact of bad news, honestly disclosed, will be lessened.

- Employees can work smarter and will work harder when they contribute to the plan and are trusted.

- Suppliers will work harder to keep your confidence and their commitments when they are trusted to contributing to customer's plans and successes.

- Customers will share their plans and reciprocate your loyalty when they know their needs are an integral part of your plans.

66

- Shareholders are more likely to believe that the Board and management can be trusted when they understand the company's direction, and are provided clear and honest reports of the company's progress.

Management walks a fine line between protecting sensitive, competitive information, and informing those who need to know the company's business. It should never discount the value of positive relationships.

Those concerned with protecting secret strategies and fearful of sharing them with employees, face a conundrum. The success of a strategy is not guaranteed by knowledge of the strategy, but by the ability to execute it successfully. Successful execution is dependent on employees having a clear understanding of the strategy in the first place. Strong internal communications help to reinforce trust, loyalty, and success.

Failing to share information creates suspicion and mistrust amongst shareholders, Directors, employees, customers, suppliers, and regulatory authorities. Those not 'in the know' tend to suspect worst-case scenarios.

- Is the company in trouble?

- Does management have ulterior motives?

- Are our jobs secure?

- Are you hiding bad financial results?

- Should suppliers be concerned about being paid?

- Are you planning to sell the company out from under us?

Secrecy is sometimes necessary, but hiding bad news or deliberately misleading shareholders or stakeholders is a separate issue. The Board should consider both as intolerable risks. Note that here, Mark has not hid bad news nor mislead anyone.

Directors who are monitoring Communications Risk should seek out and isolate the root causes of any communication failure. Those causes are usually buried in the minds and motives of those who are tasked with disseminating information.

Mark is a perfect example. He did not share his plans with the directors because he did not trust them with the information. Perhaps he lacks respect for some of them as well. Is Mark justified in his thinking? Boards can leak information. Directors, reacting to petty personal issues, can be a problem especially with not-for-profit, and 'volunteer' Boards. Directors who own shares in a corporation can act to further their own personal interests rather than the interests of the company. A CEO may have good reason not to trust the Board. Communication problems are often solved by dealing with the issues of trust and respect.

Directors need to monitor communication risk in five situations; among directors; between the Board and the CEO; with shareholders, with employees relating to the strategic plan; and with regulators. It needs to continually look for signs that the company is building and maintaining good will with its stakeholders. Taking the opportunity to speak independently with shareholders, employees, customers, suppliers, and regulators, will provide Directors with some of the information they need.

Key Points

1. The Board's only reliable source of information is the CEO.

2. Secrecy breeds suspicion and distrust. It damages relationships.

3. Communication builds trust, loyalty, good will, and good relationships. Good relationships are direct contributors to success.

4. The success of a strategy is not guaranteed by knowledge of the strategy, but rather by the ability to execute it successfully.

5. Directors monitoring Communications Risk need to seek out and isolate the root causes of communication failure.

RISK WINDOW #8 – BOARD / CEO RELATIONSHIP

Mark could have brought the Board into his thinking at an earlier stage, before his plan was complete. His action begs the question about the relationship between them.

- Was he concerned that the Board would turn him down or sabotage the plan before he had a chance to demonstrate the value in his idea?

- Is he implying that his fellow Board members are not competent to test his proposals?

- Does he think they could not be trusted with sensitive information?

- Does Mark take the Board for granted? He acts as though he controls his Board and his company.

- Is Stan Koslowsky accurate with his accusation that Mark manipulates Board members?

The relationship between the Board and CEO is the single most important factor in creating effective governance. Working together they can add considerable value to the company. Working in opposition they can rob the company of energy and insight.

An effective relationship is one of mutual accountability based on respect, trust, and candour. Boards should respect their CEOs for their ability to lead and produce results. CEOs should respect their Directors for their ability to test proposals and provide sound advice.

Boards and CEOs will only trust one another when they have demonstrated that each is trustworthy in their use of information, in their respect for each other, and in their respect for the governance process. Boards and CEOs share candour because, in passionate discussions, they have stated their ideas and opinions firmly, listened to the ideas and opinions of the others, and, when appropriate, modified their positions to create a better solution.

Accountability necessitates a relationship in a state of healthy tension. CEOs should always be conscious of their Board's ability to withhold their approval. Boards should always be concerned that, as a group, they are sufficiently competent to test their CEO's proposals and add to his strategic thinking. When the healthy tension disappears or the relationship turns sour, then the effectiveness of the Board/CEO team is at risk.

The Chair's Role

The Chair plays a special role in managing Board/CEO team risk. While Mark is responsible for making the company as competent and effective as it can be, Bill

Favro is similarly responsible for the competence, effectiveness, and continuous improvement of the Board. The chair must be concerned about:

- Creating a Board environment that will support respect, trust, and candour.

- Managing meetings that stick to the important issues and make the best use of Director's and the CEO's time

- Reminding the Board of their obligation to the company not themselves, recognizing individual vested interests, and working amongst Directors for resolution of conflicts.

- Understanding the CEO's attitude towards the Board

- Understanding the CEO's assessment of his own capacity

These are important contributions to the Board/CEO relationship that require dedicated time and focus. Their value is diluted when the CEO is also the Chair.

Key Points

1. Working together, the Board and CEO can add considerable value to the company.

2. An effective Board/CEO relationship is one of mutual accountability based on respect, trust, and candour.

3. When the healthy tension between Board and CEO disappears, then the effectiveness of the Board/CEO team is at risk.

4. The Chair has a pivotal role in managing the relationship between the Board and CEO.

WHAT ABOUT CORN BASED AVIDIN?

Ron Shendor had been waving his hand for several minutes, signalling that he wanted to speak. Finally Bill Favro acknowledged him again.

"I did some research on the internet after I received this proposal and I found that Avidin can be extracted from corn," he said. "Why haven't you covered this potential threat in your presentation? Are you withholding information from this Board that will undermine the proposal you are so intent on following?" He sat back; sure that he had caught Mark in a trap.

"Yes Ron, said Mark, we do know about corn based Avidin. Bill Sinclair's investigation identified the possibility, but we estimate the prospect to be at least ten years out with unproven economics. We believe that we can improve the economics of our process over time once it is up-and-running. Our projections show a reduction in selling price from $6000 per gram to $4500 by our ninth year of production. We think the risk of a competitor beating our selling price over the ten-year projection is less than ten percent. If corn based Avidin becomes available earlier than our ten-year projection, then the impact could be high if they are able to produce at a price lower than we are projecting." Hoping he had deflected the question, Mark sat back in his chair.

"Did he purposely leave out the reference to a competitive product," wondered Andrew as Mark spoke? "How does he calculate the ten percent risk? What is the financial impact if corn based Avidin is more than a possibility? Is this exclusion another example of Mark failing to present the whole story and all the risks to the Board? Is he being selective in what he presents in order to avoid questions he cannot easily answer? I think Ron was more prepared than Mark has bargained for."

Andrew was correct. Ron Shendor was not about to let Mark off with a simple explanation of forgetfulness. "Mark, the Internet report I read was not so pessimistic about the emergence of corm based Avidin. They are projecting a five to seven year window for significant production volumes. How do you arrive at your ten-year estimate?"

"Mr. Chair," responded Mark, "I would like Bill Sinclair to respond to Ron's question. He knows the research." And," thought Mark to himself "he had better be right one this one. I trusted his research and his judgement."

The Chair, with the consent of the board, invited Bill back to the meeting.

"Mr. Chairman." said Bill after having heard the question. "Yes, I did the research on corn based Avidin. While there are examples of optimistic projections, the actual research we examined shows there are few results on which to base any optimism. Our pilot process has produced results on which we can base a larger production process," he said, gathering confidence as he went. "If we can get the process up and running with significant production quantities at a reasonable cost, we will undercut the incentives for research on the corn based alternative. Our team is very confident that will happen."

"So you are relying on your future success to slow down a potential competitor?" asked Ron. "Isn't that a significant risk?"

"Yes," interjected Mark, taking back the floor from Bill. "I hadn't though of it in those terms, but you are correct in your reasoning Ron. I believe our assessment stands however. We can reduce the risk of competition from corn based Avidin by making sure our approach succeeds. We will review our risk assessment, however, and come back to the Board with the results."

"Ron, are you satisfied with the answer," asked Bill Favro?

"Not really," Ron said. "Once again Mark has swept the question under the rug by agreeing to bring an answer to the Board."

Andrew thought, "Another unsupported assumption to be concerned about."

The Chair excused Bill from the meeting.

A NOTE ON BUSINESS RISKS & OPPORTUNITIES

Ron Shendor has done his homework. He has drawn the Board's attention to a risk that was not mentioned in Mark's plan. He deserves credit for his question, but what about his motives? Is he acting in the best interests of the company, or is he trying to discredit Mark in order to kill the proposal and protect his own interests?

The Directors of a well-chosen Board have the advantage of coming from different backgrounds and industries, experiencing different environments, and reading different publications. They bring a wider variety of experiences and perspectives than any one CEO or management team can experience. They enrich the Board's discussion by adding different perspectives of market risks and opportunities. And they don't bring family squabbles.

While the Board should not be counted on as a routine source of industry intelligence, Directors can be valuable contributors. Information gleaned from an industry conference, or a meeting with a supplier or colleague, can provide valuable intelligence relating to customers, competitors, and suppliers.

IS THIS BOARD THE RIGHT BOARD?

"I've been on this Board longer than any of you," Richard Butler said in his slow methodical tone after being recognized by the Chair. "I've seen us grow. I've seen us change from a distributor of fresh eggs to a supplier of liquid and dried egg products to the baking and food services industry. Your parents, when they were the Directors, went through the same confrontation with Mark's father when we bought our first drying column for egg albumen. I remember. I was there. Today, we could not survive without that side of the business. We all know that the fresh egg market has little margin left in it.

"We need a full discussion of this proposal. It may be the right one, I'm not sure yet. What I am sure of is that this Board is not the right Board to carry us through the next ten years if Mark's proposal is accepted. Except for Andrew here, and Rachel, we are afraid of any risk. We are more interested in protecting our dividends than growing the company and seeing it survive in the long term. We haven't grown with the company. We don't have the skills or experience to properly assess this proposal. We don't know how to ask the critical questions about the financial risks we may be assuming, or the risks inherent in the new markets we are entering.

Mark's proposal takes into the international market with products, processes, and business risks most of us do not understand. Who is Phasor-Heston? What do they have to gain? What is the risk of using them? Are there alternatives we have not heard about? I know it won't happen overnight, but I am concerned it won't happen at all if we continue to think as we are around this table today. If Mark's proposal does nothing else, it should motivate us to acquire new Directors who can objectively assess the kinds of proposals this Board will see in the future. I believe that will be the best way we can protect our stake in our company."

Ron Shendor broke an uncomfortable moment of silence. "Speak for yourself Richard, I'm neither old nor risk averse. I just want to see this company stay on a profitable course. This proposal could ruin us."

"Well Richard," said Bill Favro, taking back the meeting, "you have an interesting perspective."

"He sure does," thought Mark as he pondered Richard's comments. "He has raised questions I didn't think we could talk about."

RISK WINDOW #9- BOARD EFFECTIVENESS

Richard Butler has identified an issue that is common for growing companies, and often goes unrecognized.

As a business grows and becomes more complex, the level of business risk grows accordingly. Complexity comes in the form of new markets, new products, larger contracts, and more sophisticated customers. It brings more stringent quality requirements and increased financing requirements. It requires additional staff, and management with new and different skills. It brings a necessity to deal with customer demands for cost reduction, and needs for more sophisticated supply chain management. If these risks are to be successfully addressed, the capacity of the CEO and the management team must grow as well.

In turn, the capacity of the Board must grow. It must be able to understand and work with the company's increasing levels of complexity and risk, to support the CEO, and to assess the CEO's ability to manage in an increasingly complex environment.

When companies first acquire a Board, the members are usually investors, family, or friends. The investors are there to protect their investment, family members are there to ensure that the CEO does not jeopardize their dividend income stream, and friends are there because they are trusted by the CEO and are more likely to support his decisions. The issue of managing complexity is rarely considered.

The complexity of Eggs Inc operations has grown considerably since its Board was first formed, but the Directors are still primarily family members. Richard Butler has concluded that the complexity of Eggs Inc. business has grown beyond his capacity, and that of some of his fellow Board members. They no longer have the ability to assess the company's risks, or to assess Mark's ability to manage those risks. They no longer have the capacity to manage effectively as Directors. It remains to be seen if they will set their egos and fears aside, and either enlarge the board, or step aside and elect a slate of outside Directors.

Maintaining an Effective Board

Effective Boards have four characteristics.

1. CEOs who recognize that Directors are allies; who bring skills and experience that compliment their own; who can assist in making difficult decisions; and who can provide the opportunity to test the CEOs ideas of direction and strategy in an environment of increasing complexity.

2. Directors who, as a group, bring a diverse range of skills and experience; have the capacity to test their CEOs' decisions; and can assess their CEOs ability to manage risk in an environment of increasing complexity.

3. An environment of respect, trust, and candour in which the Directors and the CEO recognize their effectiveness is sharpened and their power is at its peak when they are mutually dependent and equally strong.

4. A set of risk management processes and tools that bring structure and predictability to the Board's operations, and establish a process of growth, improvement, and renewal, for both the Board and the CEO.

Risk Management Processes

The Board uses five risk management processes: Strategic Planning, Management Succession, Audit, Board Effectiveness, and CEO Assessment. These processes define how the Board's work will be done and provide a clear message to the CEO that the Board is not interested in assuming a day-to-day role. They bring continuity, predictability, and discipline to the Board's deliberations. Defining the steps to be used in each process is an important way to align the thinking and expectations of the Board with the thinking and expectations of the CEO.

Mark is the greatest beneficiary of a competent Board. It's in his best interest to ensure that both he and the Board have a clear and common understanding of the step-by-step processes he will use to meet the needs and expectations of the Board. Mark after all, is the one who develops direction and strategy, and prepares the business plans. He is the one who prepares the management succession plan. He and his management team create the systems, controls, and the financial statements, that will be subjected to the audit. And he prepares all the Board material.

Preparing for Board meetings requires considerable time and effort from the management team, and deserves equal effort on the part of the Board. For its part, the Board has an obligation to be ready to discuss all Board material sent to them by the CEO. The Board also has the obligation to ensure that its members can act with independence, have the CEO's respect, are capable of testing the CEO's proposals, and have the capacity to assess the CEO's performance. It is in the Board's best interest to ensure that it has processes in place to monitor and continuously improves its own capacity and performance.

Board Process Affects Board Liability

The Board's liability for its decisions is more dependent on the quality of its decision-making process, than on its actual decisions.

The Business Judgement Rule has been developed over the years in the common Law, "...to shield from court intervention, business decisions which have been made honestly, prudently, in good faith, and on reasonable grounds. In such cases, the Board's decisions will not be subject to microscopic examination and the court will be reluctant to interfere and to usurp the Board of Director's function in managing the corporation."

The court does not judge the wisdom of the Directors decisions but rather the thoroughness of the Director's decision-making process. It is intended to protect the honest decisions of Directors and officers from a hindsight review of their unsuccessful decisions, and to refrain from stifling innovation and venturesome business activity.

Key Points

1. As a business grows and becomes more complex, the level of business risk grows accordingly. CEOs and Directors must be able to handle the increased complexity.

2. An effective Board has four components: a skilled CEO; skilled Directors; an environment of respect, trust, and candour; and effective risk management processes.

3. A Board's liability for decisions is dependent on the effectiveness of its risk management processes.

A NOTE ON BOARD INDEPENDENCE

Board independence is a fundamental prerequisite to Board effectiveness, and to the ability of the Board and CEO to act as a team. It is sufficiently important to be identified as a separate risk area for the Board to monitor.

Criteria for defining independence are published by virtually every regulatory agency. Generally they require that independent Directors:

- Not be current or former employees of the organization or related to current or former employees.

- Have no material relationship to the organization. (Generally defined as and material dealing with the organization, or direct material compensation in the form of salaries, or fees, other than Director's fees.)

- Not be related to the CEO *or controlling shareholder.*

Most of these criteria are structural in nature, but the real test of independence is not structural but behavioural.

It's not who Directors are but how they act, that counts. Directors should be free to act independently of the CEO and each other without regard for repercussion. Directors should express opinions and vote based on their impartial appraisal of an issue and not at the dictate of the CEO, another Director, or a shareholder.

Independence encourages Directors to challenge management's decisions and evaluate corporate performance from a completely free and objective perspective. It encourages open dissent, and the freedom to challenge each other's assumptions, beliefs, and positions. Independence is an important aspect of the healthy tension that sharpens management's analysis, enhances accountability, and leads to better decisions by management and the Board.

Independence Is a Challenge for SMEs

Independence is a difficult goal for SMEs, and Eggs Inc. is no exception. Directors are supposed to act in the best interests of the company and all its shareholders. But Eggs Inc. Directors are also shareholders with their own vested interests.

Mark's interests are centred on growth and control—control he has not shown any sign of surrendering as a member of the family that sees Eggs Inc. as a Springfield family business.

A predictable stream of dividend income is the dominant interest of several Directors. Their quarterly dividend cheques support their lifestyles. They will support strategies for growth so long as they do not affect their cash flow.

If Ian Black of Equity Partners Inc. joins the Board, he will endeavour to favour his company's interests. As a part of the agreement to purchase Eggs Inc. shares, he will insist on a business plan that supports his company's objectives. He will require the Board to approve a Unanimous Shareholder's Agreement that protects his company's ability to sell its shares in seven years with a thirty percent return on investment. He will monitor Mark's progress against the business plan to ensure it is being followed. As the time approaches for his company to exit and sell its shares, his focus will narrow and become more short term as he works to ensure the greatest share value and the least perceived risk to potential new investors.

The Board should openly recognize and acknowledge these conflicting interests. If they are out in the open, then the positions taken by individual directors during Board discussions can be more readily understood, and the issues they create, more readily resolved.

Independence is not a guarantee

Independence by itself is not a guarantee of effectiveness. Independence must be accompanied by skills, knowledge, and experience, equal to the situation. Eggs Inc. Directors probably meet the criteria for independence. But as Richard Butler has suggested, the Directors may not be skilled enough given the increased complexity of the business.

Of course, there are always exceptions to the rule, and some companies do exceedingly well without demonstrating independence. Many companies score poorly on the indexes used to judge independence but demonstrate exceptional growth in share value.

In most instances however, independent Boards will create greater value than those that do not demonstrate independence.

Key Points

1. Board independence is a fundamental prerequisite to Board effectiveness, and to the ability of the Board and CEO to act as a team.

2. The real test of independence is whether Directors are free to act independently of the CEO and each other without regard for repercussion.

3. Many Directors have conflicting interests.

THE DISCUSSION

The questioning to this point had been as Mark anticipated. Now he felt it was time to put one more item on the table.

"Bill," he said to the Chair, "I have a further comment."

"Go ahead Mark," responded Bill. "You have the floor."

Mark began, "We have not shared with you the alternatives considered before settling on the one presented today. We examined three different scenarios. One was to expand our current business to a national scale by aggressively buying up our five main competitors. It could be done, but we would be paying top dollar and we would be left with trying to integrate five companies into one. We have good management but we don't have the strength to accomplish that task. As you know from the conventions we have attended, most of our competitors are far weaker in management than we are. We could not expect to acquire additional management strength from them.

"The second alternative was to sell out to Braxton, our major competitor in the southwest. They are on the acquisition trail. They approached us last March, as I told you. Some of you may have preferred to take their offer and get out all together. That would have given us money in our pockets but they were not offering a fair price given our place in the industry.

"We rejected that idea because, in the long run our third alternative, the enzyme extraction business, will prove to be far more profitable for the company and its shareholders. There is more risk to be sure, but also considerably greater reward for those who have the courage to stay in the game. We all have to make the decision to stay or fold."

Mark sat down to silence. While he had not offered to buy them out, it was clear that he had a buy out in mind if necessary.

It was also clear that Mark intended to proceed with the project whether some directors liked it or not. He was counting on the nay-sayers fear that they might lose out on something big. They were scared, but they also liked the income and the lifestyle the company had brought under the Springfield family leadership.

"So much for consensus," said Stan Koslowsky. "You are no different than your father and grandfather."

Mark noted that he did not offer to tender his shares.

"So, what are you asking of us today?" Andrew Benson asked. "We still have some unanswered questions. We don't have a final set of budget numbers for the construction and capital equipment. We don't have the downside analysis. We don't have clarity on the deal with the University. You have work to do on a new IT system. And we need more information on corn-based

Avidin. What do you expect the Board to do given these issues?"

"I'm looking for the Board's agreement to proceed with phase one of the plan. My five motions are included in the Board material," said Mark. "They are:

1. Approve the plan in principle, as presented

2. Approve the expenditure of $500,000 to proceed with phase one trials in conjunction with the University's Research Development Fund and to prepare the preliminary design for the phase-two plant.

3. Agree to the sale of 25% of Eggs Inc to Equity partners Inc. for $7 Million.

4. Agree to the sale of 5% of Eggs Inc. to the University Research Development Fund.

5. Approve the expansion of the Board to nine members, two of which are to be named by Equity Partners Inc.

"So far we have been working from estimates. The next part will be more expensive. The pilot plant studies at the University will become more intensive. And the financials will become more accurate."

Ron Shendor leapt into the discussion. "Why do we need an equity partner? What do they add? It seems to me that we are simply going to piggyback on our success and then walk away with our money. And what if your scheme fails? They will own 25% of the company. Is that a risk we want to take?"

"That's a bit unfair Ron," said Mark. "Without our equity partner we would be required to reduce our dividend distribution down to a mere trickle for about three and a half years. I didn't think our shareholders would like that option so I looked for a source of equity rather than debt. Ian's company seemed like they were most easy to work with and would add to our Board's capability. I thought the benefits outweigh the risks in this case."

"There you go again," yelled Stan. "Buying us with our own money. Of course your thoughtful gesture will win some members over to your side."

Mark thought, "Stan, you are your own worst enemy and my best friend. If you were cool about your objections, you might be more effective in winning support from the Board."

Andrew signalled his intention to speak. "Go ahead Andrew," said Bill Favro.

"This decision comes down to deciding whether the level of risk inherent in Mark's proposal, is acceptable to the Board. As I see it, we are looking at three major risks; the risk of entering the enzyme business; the risk of changing our entire information system at the same time as we are building a new product line; and the risk of being successful enough to discourage a corn-based supplier from entering the market. This proposal assumes that the company has the capacity to do all three successfully and at the same time. Are we not increasing our risk by an order of magnitude if we try?"

"I think that is a legitimate question," said Rachel Adams, "but one for which we do not have an answer today. But do we need to have the answer today?

Mark's proposal is very attractive at half the return. He is asking for the Board's approval to start us down the path to answering the questions that he and this Board have raised. The three phases will give us the opportunity to shut down the project and limit our losses if the answers are not forthcoming, or are not within the risk parameters we set as limits. We do need Mark's assurance that we will be fully informed of progress in a timely manner, that he will address the questions raised in today's meeting, and that he will have the good sense to recommend pulling the plug if he sees that his objectives cannot be met."

"You have my assurance," said Mark.

Richard Butler raised his hand. "Mr. Chairman, we have a motion on the table. I suggest we have the vote"

"It seems that all the questions have been asked so the vote is in order," said Bill Favro. "All in favour of the motion to proceed with phase one of Mark's proposal?" He glanced around the table. Five hands were raised.

"All against?" No hands.

"I want the minutes to show that I abstained in protest," said Stan Koslowsky. "Me too," chimed in Ron.

MARK'S SECOND BOMBSHELL

After the vote Mark was recognized by the Chair and stood up. "I am grateful that we reached consensus today. Thank you for showing faith in me, our management, our advisors, and in this idea. I must tell you however that I intend to resign as CEO within eighteen months."

"What," shouted Stan Koslowsky? "You got us into this new plan and now you are telling us you can't manage it? Have you sold us down the river? Bill, can we have a re-vote?"

"Mark has the floor," commanded the Chair. "Let's hear him out."

"No Stan," said Mark, "I haven't sold you down the river. In fact I've done just the opposite. I've set this company on a new and promising course and I've also had the courage and the decency to acknowledge that a better leader than me is required to make it work for us all in the long term. Remember Stan; my family has more money in this company than yours does. I would not bet on anything I did not believe would be a winner, and I will not let my own ego spoil the bet. Richard Butler was right. I do not think we are the right Board for the next phase of Egg's Inc life and I know I am not the right CEO. Our business is becoming more complex. Our entry into the enzyme extraction business will add a new dimension to our company. The increasing competition and cost pressure we are facing in our traditional markets will require more focus on making us a leaner operation. These pressures are already being addressed in the other manufacturing industries and they are coming to the food industry as well. These are challenges I am not equipped to manage. As Eggs Inc. grows my limitations will become exaggerated. This new venture will take the company beyond my real capacity. I have been grooming a successor, as all of you know. My daughter Christine has worked with Eggs Inc. for several years now. She has both the education and the management foresight to manage the larger entity. She has been the brain behind the extraction project and I am convinced that she understands the situation we are getting into."

"The dynasty continues," groaned Stan.

Mark continued. "That being said, I think we need to divorce ourselves from the era of family ties, as Richard has suggested. I believe that if Christine is to lead this organization, she must emerge from a proper search as the best candidate for the job. Mr. Chairman, I move that we begin the search for a new CEO. The first step will be to hire a search firm to help us in the identification and selection of a candidate. I expect the task will require twelve months to complete."

"Hmm," thought Andrew Benson to himself, "That adds another major risk, a new CEO."

RISK WINDOW #10 – CEO CAPACITY

Mark has recognized his own limitations. He has a strong track-record of success in building Eggs Inc, but he has acknowledged to himself and his Board, that the company will be more prosperous in the long run under different leadership. He has acknowledged that to protect what he and his family have built, he must step down in favour of a new CEO who has the capacity to lead the company into the future. He has made his decision despite his strong inclination to be in control.

In Fortune 500 companies, CEO's are routinely removed by their Boards. The average life of a Fortune 500 CEO is said to be between 2 and 4 years.

For SMEs however, the issue is very different. They are usually closely held by one person or by a family. The CEO is often the founder or builder of the company who sees the company as his life's work. The idea of relinquishing control is usually alien. When the company grows to a level beyond their ability to accommodate and manage the complexity of the business most are unable to see, or are reluctant to admit, their own limitations.

Managing Complexity

The idea of differing abilities to manage complexity was introduced by Elliott Jaques in his book, "Executive leadership, A Practical Guide To Managing Complexity," written with Stephen D. Clement.[1] Complexity, they say, is a function of the time span for which decisions must be made, the magnitude of the issues being addressed, and the number of variables to be managed.

To manage complexity requires the CEO to:

1. Create clarity from a confusing mass of issues and problems by simplifying them down to the few critical root issues that will determine success, and for which decisions can be made

2. Conceiving a strategy for dealing with the root issues, and communicating it to the organization using a plan that is seen as being achievable by those who are held accountable for it goals.

The ability to extract clarity and simplicity from confusion is not a universal talent. All CEOs and Directors are not endowed with the same capacity to understand and manage complexity. Most can manage at low levels. Fewer can manage as the level of complexity increases. To manage the risk of CEO capacity, the Board itself must have the capacity to manage at increasing levels of complexity.

Managing the CEO Capacity Risk

As the Board cycles annually though it's five, risk management processes, it is given the opportunity to continuously observe the CEO's ability to manage complexity in eight risk windows.

- Direction, Strategy and Goals
- Security and Use Of Assets
- Management Strength
- Communication
- Financial Strength
- Regulatory Issues
- Financial systems & Controls
- Board/CEO Relationship

Concerns for the CEO's ability to manage complexity are not revealed to the Board in a blinding flash. They come over time. They come as subtle observations of trends in behaviour, made by individual Board members, who notice that the CEO is having difficulty getting a particular problem under control.

Nor does the CEO recognize his/her limitations in a blinding flash. They come over time, as they notice they are having difficulty in seeing through the fog of problems, or developing a new plan. They may not recognize the problem, but they will show their frustration.

In the chapter describing *"Risk Window #2 - Management Strength,"* we saw the value of discussing Director observations at the end of each Board meeting. Observations of CEO difficulties are the most difficult to voice. No director wants to be seen as unfairly questioning the competence of the CEO. But these are the circumstances in which the Board's values of respect, trust, and candour, allow Directors to comment without prejudice, about what they observe. Trends, caught early, can lead to simple and inexpensive solutions. If the CEO is slipping, then the Board could provide mentorship that might solve the problem. If the problem is allowed to grow, salvaging the situation could require the CEO's replacement.

The Board is rarely anxious to contemplate a change in leadership. It's one of the most significant risks the Board will encounter. It requires time, and a successful outcome is not guaranteed. Poorly handled it can weaken the company in the marketplace.

CEO succession is difficult for entrepreneurial companies managed by the owner/founder. Helping the CEO, who is often the majority shareholder, to recognize that he/she is no longer able to lead the company, requires tact, time, and clear evidence to demonstrate the reality of the situation.

Key Points

1. Corporate growth brings complexity to the issues and problems that both Board and CEO must manage.

2. The CEO's capacity to manage as complexity of the business increases, is a significant issue for the Board to monitor.

[1]   "Executive leadership, A Practical Guide to Managing Complexity," Elliott Jaques and Stephen D. Clement, Cason Hall & Co., 1991

HOW DO MARK AND HIS BOARD RATE?

GovernanceTools™ segments the Board's risk assessment problem into the twelve categories we have described in this book. Eight of the risk categories are related to the CEO's capacity to manage. Three are related to the Board's capacity to function as a risk management unit, and one, the Board/CEO Relationship Risk, is common to both.

Direction and strategy – Mark's proposal to the Directors was weak. It lacked a description of the assumptions made, and the alternatives considered. It lacked an analysis of the market for Avidin and Lysozyme. It did not include an assessment of the downside risk.

Perhaps the omissions occurred because Mark believed his Board would not understand them. Perhaps they were made because he did not believe he needed to work very hard to get support for his proposal from a Board he virtually controlled. Either way, he was remiss. His plan was not tested by the Board, as it should have been. The project will proceed at greater risk than is either necessary or appropriate.

Management strength – Mark appears to have a developed a strong management team and has recognized the risks to management strength that his proposal represents. The fact that one of his Board members, Rachel Adams, identified a potential risk area and made a useful suggestion for improvement should not be taken as a weakness in Mark's management, but rather a valuable contribution to the risk assessment by a Board member. In this case Rachel assessed the risk appropriately. Mark will examine his plan and better manage the risk.

Financial Strength – Mark did not present a downside analysis showing the effects if his proposal failed. He may believe the chances of failure to be minimal, but they should have been given to the Board as assurance that he had considered them. Andrew Benson asked appropriate questions.

Financial Systems and Controls – Mark has clearly considered this risk and has identified a risk management strategy. He will implement a new IT system. But, he has allowed the existing financial system to deteriorate to the point where the auditor commented on it in his notes. It should never have reached that point. As well, he did not recognize the challenges he will face in implementing a new system. Again, the experience of a Director has added to the management of risk for this project and for the company.

Security and use of assets – Mark has considered the continued operation of the egg products side of the business although he may have been naive in his assessment of demands on his time.

Regulatory compliance – Mark has clearly identified the risks associated with regulatory compliance and factored them into his plan.

Communication – Mark kept his Board in the dark about his new direction. Even the Chair was not appraised of his intentions. He has left us with the impression that he may have purposely left out critical information about corn-based Avidin, a competitive process. These are serious issues. Were they the result of the Board's weakness, or Mark's arrogance? The communication problem is systemic, a result of the Board's weakness and Mark's belief that he will achieve the Board's approval regardless. Major change is required to fix this situation of this magnitude.

CEO's Leadership Capacity – Mark has identified the most crucial issue for the company, his capacity to lead into the future. He knows that he has done well in the past but acknowledges that his ability to perform in the future is the issue. The Board did not have the capacity to critically assess this weakness.

Board Effectiveness –It's clear that Eggs Inc. has grown beyond the Board's capacity to effectively assess Mark's proposals or his capabilities. Mark did make some effort to enhance their capability by adding Andrew Benson. But Andrew has not been properly coached in his responsibilities. He should have been more forthcoming in his assessment of Mark's proposal and its lack of detail. The critical factor however, is that the Board has no mechanism to judge its own effectiveness.

Business risks and opportunities – With the exception of Rachel and Andrew, the Directors are not well linked to other business environments. They have little opportunity to observe events that could be opportunities or risks to Eggs Inc. Note that both Rachel and Andrew drew on their outside experiences.

Board/CEO relationship – It is clear that the relationship between Mark and some of his Board members has deteriorated and that the situation has been allowed to persist. The Chair should have recognized and addressed it.

Board independence – The traditional means of demonstrating independence is that each Director makes their decisions in the best interests of the company, without being unduly influenced by the CEO or each other. On the surface Eggs Inc Directors appear independent but, because several of the Directors do not have a real capability for judging Mark's proposal, their independence is more illusory than real and they default to serving their own vested interests.

Eggs Inc. Board is ripe for change

Eggs Inc is entering a period of transition, common to growing companies, where the best interests of the company and its shareholders are not best served by the Board and CEO that made it successful in the past.

With two exceptions, the Directors do not bring skills and experience that compliment Mark's, or who provide a forum capable of testing his ideas of direction and strategy. Mark does not regard the Directors as allies, but rather as a group that needs to be manipulated if he is to get his own way. The Directors are unable to observe Mark's deficiencies in handling complexity.

Mark, by his own admission, is not able to manage the complexity that he knows will accompany the growth and expansion of Eggs Inc. His admission is noteworthy, but he has not worked with his Board to help them to understand the company's risk exposure more clearly.

Mark's initiative to resign has placed Eggs Inc. in a position where the transition may be successful. Many Boards and CEOs do not recognize the situation and fail to take advantage of their potential.

EPILOGUE

The Board meeting started a chain of events that dramatically altered the character of Eggs Inc. and its Board. Richard Butler's comments on Board effectiveness and Mark's resignation brought the issue of change to the forefront and the Board acted quickly.

The change started with the acquisition of a new CEO. Aided by an outside advisor, the Board's search committee quickly discovered Malcolm Ridley. He was an experienced CEO of a small pharmaceutical company who had engineered the merger of his firm with another, larger company. He had lost out in the subsequent contest for CEO of the new entity. Eggs Inc. was much smaller than his previous company, but the challenge of bringing Avidin to production, and the opportunity to build a company, won him over. "He is exceptionally talented," Mark was quoted as saying when interviewed by the Free Press, "and we believe that Eggs Inc. will grow substantially under his leadership."

Christine, Mark's daughter was one of the contenders for Mark's job. After interviewing the other candidates, it became clear that she lacked the experience to be a strong candidate. Malcolm was offered the job.

However Christine's knowledge of the new plant and her genuine capabilities impressed Malcolm and she was appointed Vice-President in charge of the new enzyme operation. She was happy to learn under Malcolm's tutelage.

Mark agreed to stay on as an advisor for six months to assist Malcolm in the transition. But it soon became clear that Malcolm had the vision and the skill to take the helm and move quickly. Mark declined to become Chairman of the Board, even though his share ownership and his influence with other shareholders could have guaranteed him the post. He confided to Rachel his realization that having strong Directors representing the family's interests was better than having direct control.

With the search complete and Malcolm firmly in charge, Stan Koslowsky and Ron Shendor resigned from the Board. They had initially suspected that Richard Butler's speech and Mark's resignation were a conspiracy to get them off the Board, but as the search progressed they realized Mark's appraisal of his capabilities was sincere. They resigned, along with Richard Butler, six months after Malcolm took over. By that time the Board had identified three new prospective Board members who were a match for Malcolm's ability.

Rachel stayed on the Board with Mark's encouragement. Mark was convinced she had the capacity to serve the Board effectively and besides, he told her, "What better way to boost your own management skills and serve your own business. You will be rubbing shoulders with some great people." He was right.

The new Board jelled quickly and Rachel was enthusiastic in her praise for its effectiveness. "Malcolm uses us as a sounding Board," she told Mark one day over lunch. "The discussion is often intense and was a bit intimidating for me at first. It took me a while to recognize that these are strong people, passionately expressing their views, and expecting the rest of us to do the same. We seem to get to the heart of an issue very quickly and usually come up with a resolution that is better than want we started with. Bill Favro has blossomed as the Chair. He is a great moderator and has earned the Board's respect."

Mark's services as a Director are still in great demand. He told his Daughter Christine that being an outside Director was more difficult than he had thought. "It was hard for me to forget trying to be the CEO and instead be an advisor and risk manager," he confessed over a family dinner, "but I am learning."

Eggs Inc. was successful in developing the enzyme extraction process although it took six months longer and cost 20% more than Mark's original forecast. The good news was that the process efficiency proved to be much higher than expected so the long-term profitability far exceeded expectations. Christine was instrumental in recognizing that other enzymes could be extracted from albumen using the same process. Eggs Inc was soon a source of several valuable products that greatly enhanced the bottom line and Eggs Inc. access to egg supplies. The competition from corn-based Avidin did materialize, but was not a major issue.

As the date for Equity Partners Inc share redemption approached, an international food services company

CONTENTS

INTRODUCTION

It was a hot summer night in Fort Sumner, New Mexico, when outlaw Billy the Kid arrived there in 1881. Billy had been running from Sheriff Pat Garrett for months, after escaping from a jail in Lincoln, New Mexico. Garrett had chased Billy across 140 miles (225 kilometers) of harsh, dangerous desert. Now, Garrett had finally caught up to the young outlaw.

Billy the Kid had been jailed for killing people and stealing horses. The determined Sheriff Garrett believed that Billy would be a threat to others unless he was captured again. The deadly confrontation that night between these two men would become part of the history of the Old West and an important piece of American folklore.

Lawmen often formed posses to capture outlaws. This posse aboard a train is going after the Wild Bunch, one of the most famous groups of outlaws.

Throughout the second half of the nineteenth century, America's western frontier was rapidly growing. In 1848, the gold rush attracted people from all over the world. Others came from the East to start new lives in the wide, open western territories. Most people lived honestly. But some men and women were willing to do anything for money—even steal or kill. Other Americans wanted to make the frontier a safer home for new settlers. They were willing to give their lives to tame these lands.

The struggle between lawmen and outlaws would determine how life would be lived in America's Wild West.

When Billy the Kid escaped from jail, posters, such as this one, offered rewards to anyone who could turn him in—dead or alive!

REWARD
($5,000.00)

Reward for the capture, dead or alive, of one Wm. Wright, better known as

"BILLY THE KID"

Age, 18. Height, 5 feet, 3 inches. Weight, 125 lbs. Light hair, blue eyes and even features. He is the leader of the worst band of desperadoes the Territory has ever had to deal with. The above reward will be paid for his capture or positive proof of his death.

JIM DALTON, Sheriff.

DEAD OR ALIVE!
"BILLY THE KID"

OCCUPATION FOR RAINY DAYS.

A PLEASANT SURPRISE.

SCENES AT THE GOLD DIGGINGS.

n the page herewith we present five pictures so expressive and racteristic, that but few words are required by way of explana-. The series tell a connected story at a glance. The first ure represents the nner in which the l diggers of Cali-nia are accustomed occupy themselves a rainy day, viz., mending their hes, and repairing r boots and tools a-door occupation, a very necessary y. The second ure is rather a lu-rous one, and rep-ents an interior w of a man's cab-which has been en possession of by of the numerous rs that abound in diggings, and which ning to have re-ed itself sufficiently the stores of the in is now seen warm-itself, after the style human being across hair. The third, centre picture, is a fine and expres-one, representing miners engaged in ghing the dust ch has cost them so ch labor to procure. tools of their call-are strewn upon table before them, ng utensils, fire-s and scales. One enjoying his pipe, another looks on ghtfully at the op-tion of weighing formed by his com-e. The fourth pic-, below, represents miners engaged in forming their culi-y duty. One is ac-ly engaged over

per, and consequently, as these hardy sons of toil have plenty of appetite, we must suppose that their sauce is of the choicest sort. The fifth and last picture, represents the miners washing their clothing on the river's bank, and hanging the clothes to dry on

idea of profit by the obtaining of gold, has its cha must confess that we do not wonder that a feeling o ter should possess many a stout heart and gallan very flower of New England youth—that is to say,

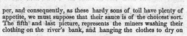

REPRESENTATION OF MINERS WEIGHING THEIR GOLD.

fire, with the food, the savory smell of which attracts the dog d by, who eyes it wishfully, while the other miner is pounding corn with a pestle and mortar, to make a pudding with which nish the meal. Hunger is said to be the best sauce for sup-

the branches of the trees. Their wants are simple and easily sup-plied. They require neither starching nor ironing for their coarse under clothes, and they are quickly cleansed and ready for use without the laundress's care. To many this life, aside from the

sinew—ha to the sho cific, in a shining r adventure before ta to remar very few f who do n or more their circ the gold California The con this imm of manua to the pu ing, is to the yield the mort country, vast numl tutions, And while enriched the scenes hood, a die at a c friends a Many phi say that of gold in in reality, than a ble adduce al gent evils sulted fron but forge cannot di den purpo Providenc thus reve to men's ways of P inscrutable can fathor that the gold in C Australia some goo

yond its apparent application, we have not the shado It seems to have been reserved till this day, as on auxiliary in bringing the whole world under the infl ilization and religion.

MINERS PREPARING THEIR FOOD.

MINERS WASHING THEIR CLOTHING.

CHAPTER 1

DISTURBING THE PEACE

The Dreamers

On a cold morning in January 1848, James Marshall found a few pieces of gold in a riverbed at Sutter's Fort. Sutter's Fort was a sawmill near Sacramento, California. Marshall swiftly went to tell John Sutter, the owner of the sawmill, about his discovery.

The news of Marshall's discovery spread quickly. People from all over the world flocked to California to strike it rich. One-half million people came to the area during the gold rush! The gold rush marked the beginning of the Wild West.

Most of the treasure seekers of the gold rush headed for California in 1849. These people were called forty-niners.

· FRONTIER FACT ·

Buffalo Bill Cody made up the term *Wild West*. Buffalo Bill was a cowboy and sharpshooter of the 1800s who toured the country with his Wild West show.

In the early days of the gold rush, there was little crime. That was because there was plenty of gold and land. As more people came to look for gold, towns and mining camps became very crowded.

There was no police force to protect and defend the mining camps where most prospectors lived and mined. Some prospectors carried a gun for protection. Other men used guns to steal gold, horses, and food. After work, many miners spent their money drinking and gambling in the saloons. These saloons were very dangerous. The combination of alcohol, money, and guns often led to violent deaths for many.

Vigilante Justice

Rising crime and violence concerned many people of California. They did not want to live in fear. Since there was no police force, cities formed vigilante groups. A vigilante is a person who takes the law into his or her own hands by capturing and punishing suspected criminals.

One of the most famous vigilante groups was the San Francisco Committee of Vigilance, formed in the 1850s. A committee is a group of people who make decisions for a larger group. About eight thousand men joined this committee. The group captured and punished dozens of suspected criminals. Although the group helped stop some crimes, it began to lose public support. Many people in California came to believe that vigilante justice was unfair. They often wondered if the vigilante groups were sometimes punishing innocent people.

Joaquín Murrieta

Of course, many men and women from the gold rush era *were* proven criminals. One of the most famous outlaws from that time period was Joaquín (**wha**-keen) Murrieta. Murrieta was born in Mexico in 1828. In 1850, he went to California. He claimed a piece of land, hoping to find gold on it.

But American miners mistreated members of Murrieta's family. His brother was convicted of stealing a horse and was hung. Days later, Murrieta's wife was assaulted. Murrieta went to file charges, but the county

Some people came to see Joaquín Murrieta as a hero who stood up against racism. John Rollin Ridge published Joaquín Murrieta: A Celebrated California Bandit *in 1854.*

sheriff did not help him. Eventually, Murrieta was driven from his land.

A Secret Pact

Murrieta believed these actions against his family were racist. He decided to fight back against the attacks. He formed a secret pact with fellow Mexicans. These Mexicans also felt threatened by racism and swore to get—or take—whatever they wanted in California. Their motto was "All or nothing." The fierce gang had twenty-two members. They stole horses, raided mining camps, and stole gold from miners. From 1850 to 1853, the gang killed forty-one people.

Local newspapers usually credited the crimes simply to "Joaquín." However, there were five men named Joaquín in the gang. This made knowing which crimes Murrieta himself was responsible for difficult.

Catch Him If You Can

The government of California was determined to stop Murrieta and his gang. They created a special police force, the California Rangers, to capture him. In May 1853, the hunt began. Captain Harry Love led the California Rangers. The Rangers searched for Murrieta for two months. In July, they finally uncovered his trail. He was leading a herd of stolen horses south to Mexico. After several days of tracking the trail, the Rangers surprised a group of thirty Mexican horsemen. Some of them were members of Murrieta's gang.

A bloody shoot-out and chase followed. Ranger Harry Love shot and killed Murrieta. At least Love *thought* that he had gunned down Murrieta. Love wanted to prove that he had killed the famous outlaw. To do this, he chopped off Murrieta's head and took it back to Sacramento, California. The head had blue eyes and brown hair. However, wanted posters showed Murrieta as having black hair and brown eyes. There were no existing photographs of Murrieta, so there was no way to prove his identity.

THE LEGEND OF JOAQUÍN MURRIETA

As late as 1856, newspapers reported that eyewitnesses had seen Murrieta alive in Mexico. To this day, no one has been able to prove that Harry Love killed Joaquín Murrieta. Also to this day, some people still think of Murrieta as a hero. These people believe Murrieta was a man who fought back against racism. Many others, though, thought Murrieta was a dangerous, bloodthirsty bandit who killed many innocent people.

CHAPTER 2

BIG CRIMES IN THE BOOMTOWNS

The American Civil War was fought between the Confederacy, or Southern states, and the Union, or Northern states, from 1861 until 1865. Many men joined to fight in the armies of the Northern or Southern states. Therefore, during the war, fewer people traveled to frontier lands in the western part of America.

After the war, many people moved west again. Some became cowboys, earning their living by taking care of and herding cattle on ranches. Others moved to the gold and silver mines. Many small mining camps quickly became large towns. These boomtowns were the settings for many scenes of violence.

The silver rush in Tombstone, Arizona, brought about seven thousand people to the area by 1881. Here residents gather outside of the Tombstone Epitaph, *the town newspaper, for this photograph taken in 1885.*

17

Tombstone, Arizona, was a classic Western boomtown. It sprang up in 1878 near the site where an ex-soldier had found silver. The town attracted many different kinds of people, including silver miners, businessmen, and cowboys. All came searching for a better life.

Wyatt Earp

Tombstone was known for being a wild, violent town. Saloons popped up on almost every street. Tough lawmen were needed to keep the peace. Wyatt Earp was the most famous Tombstone peace officer. He was born in Illinois in 1848. At the age of sixteen, he moved with his family to California. He drove freight wagons and worked for a railroad there.

Wyatt Earp's adventurous life has been the inspiration for many books and movies.

In 1879, Wyatt moved to Tombstone with his brother Virgil. Virgil became a deputy U.S. marshal. Wyatt was named the town's deputy sheriff. Soon, two more of Wyatt's brothers, Morgan and Warren, also settled in Tombstone. The townspeople were impressed by the Earp brothers' fairness as lawmen. They were serious about keeping Tombstone free from crime.

·FRONTIER FACT·

Virgil once arrested Wyatt for disturbing the peace! After the arrest, Wyatt calmly paid the twenty-dollar fine.

Doc Holliday

One of Wyatt's close friends was another famous gunslinger. His name was Doc Holliday. Holliday was born John Henry Holliday in Georgia in 1851. At age twenty, he became a dentist. Shortly after finishing dental school, Holliday got sick with tuberculosis. This disease affected his lungs. His doctors suggested that he move to a drier climate.

Holliday moved to Dallas, Texas, in 1872. There, he became interested in gambling. At first, it was only a hobby. However, Holliday eventually gave up dentistry. He began to travel and gamble throughout the West. During one of his gambling trips, Holliday met Wyatt Earp. The two became good friends. In 1880, Holliday packed up and moved to Tombstone. He continued to gamble there, while also spending lots of his time with Wyatt Earp.

The O.K. Corral

The cowboys in Tombstone were a rough bunch. The businessmen of the town often accused the cowboys of robbing their stagecoaches. There was great tension between the two groups. The Earp brothers usually sided with the businessmen. Because of this, the cowboys saw the Earps as enemies. Meanwhile, Tombstone's head sheriff, John Behan, took the cowboys' side.

This photograph was taken in 1885, four years after the gunfight between the Earps and the cowboys.

The cowboys threatened to kill Doc Holliday and the Earps. For nearly two years, no blood was spilled, but tension between the two sides grew. On October 26, 1881, the Earp brothers and Doc Holliday decided to put an end to the cowboys' threats. They cornered the cowboys near the O.K. Corral. The Earp brothers yelled at the cowboys to throw their hands up.

The cowboys threw their hands up, all right, but they were holding and firing their pistols. Gunshots rang out from both sides. In a matter of seconds, the fight was over. Three cowboys lay dead. Virgil and Morgan

Earp were wounded. This gunfight is the most famous in Wild West history. It also marked the beginning of a bloody feud.

Five months later, the cowboys cornered Morgan Earp in a pool hall. They shot him dead. Wyatt swore revenge. Until then, Wyatt had worked within the law. Now, he was about to go on a hunt that would brand him as the most notorious lawman in the West. Wyatt and Doc Holliday killed five men. Sheriff Behan arrested Earp, but Wyatt's businessmen friends bailed him out of jail.

Billy the Kid

Lincoln, New Mexico, was another famous boomtown. It was created in 1849. By the late 1870s, Lincoln had become a dangerous place to live. There was also serious competition for business. John Chisum and John Tunstall were fiercely competing with Lawrence Murphy and James Dolan for control of business in Lincoln.

In 1877, Billy the Kid moved to Lincoln County. Little is known for sure about Billy the Kid's short life. He remains a mysterious figure in Wild West folklore. Some historians have tried to piece together his life. Many details, however, are still unclear.

Historians believe Billy was born in New York in 1859. They think his birth name was Henry McCarty. At age fourteen, Henry and his mother may have moved to New Mexico. A year later, his mother died. At that time, Henry changed his name to William H. Bonney.

Billy the Kid has been described as very friendly and kind in his treatment of people who were not his enemies.

When Billy moved to Lincoln, John Tunstall hired him as a rider to help protect his cattle. In February 1878, Murphy's group killed Tunstall. The Lincoln County War had begun. Billy vowed to avenge Tunstall's murder. Billy and his fellow ranch workers were made deputies. Their job was to arrest Tunstall's killers. Billy had a different plan, though. He and his gang, the Regulators, killed several of Murphy's associates. Billy also killed Lincoln's Sheriff Brady and fled. The newspapers dubbed Billy "the Kid" because of his age. Popular belief is that he was only nineteen at the time.

The war came to a head in July 1878. The Regulators heard that Murphy's men had sworn to kill Alex McSween, a friend of Tunstall. They rushed back to Lincoln. Murphy's group surrounded McSween's house on July 19. Inside the house, Billy and his gang fought back, until Murphy's men set the house on fire. Billy and the Regulators escaped, but McSween and several others were shot.

The Kid's Last Stand

In 1879, Billy was arrested for Sheriff Brady's murder, but he escaped from jail. In December 1880, Lincoln's new sheriff, Pat Garrett, caught him. In April 1881, Billy was sentenced to die. He was moved from Santa Fe, New Mexico, to the Lincoln County jail. Billy managed to escape before his execution. Sheriff Pat Garrett hunted him for about two months.

Most historians believe that Billy the Kid met his end in Fort Sumner, New Mexico, on July 14. When Pat Garrett and his two deputies reached Fort Sumner, they went to see Pete Maxwell. Garrett thought Billy might try to hide at Maxwell's house. Garrett sat talking quietly to Maxwell in his dark bedroom. His two deputies waited outside. Billy the Kid walked up to the deputies and asked who they were. According to most accounts, these were the last words Billy the Kid would ever say. Garrett recognized Billy's voice and fired his gun, killing Billy the Kid. The outlaw was only twenty-two years old.

CHAPTER 3

GANGS, GUNS, AND THE LAW

The James Gang

Banks and trains became popular targets for outlaws during the 1870s. To the Western criminal, these were obvious places where lots of money and valuables could be found. Jesse James was the Wild West's first famous bank robber.

Jesse James was born in Missouri in 1847. During the Civil War, Jesse and his brother Frank joined a band of Southern fighters. He was only sixteen years old. The group of fighters the James brothers joined was not an official part of the Confederate army. However, they did work to weaken and harm the Union army. They often raided and robbed Northern-owned banks. Jesse was shot several times during the war.

Jesse James (left) is shown here with members of his gang. In September 1876, the James brothers and their gang tried to rob the First National Bank in Northfield, Minnesota. Eight members of the James gang were killed. Only the James brothers survived. **27**

After the war ended, the brothers and their gang continued their raids. Their raids were now considered robberies instead of acts of war. The James gang was accused of over two dozen robberies from 1869 to 1871. The gang boldly held up banks in broad daylight. They shot and killed six men during these early robberies.

It Gets Personal

The James gang began robbing trains in 1873. They piled rocks on the train tracks, forcing trains to stop. Then they robbed the passengers of purses, wallets, and jewels. They also raided the trains' safes, which usually contained thousands of dollars. The James gang was wanted in six states, yet no one was able to catch them.

These outlaws became the nation's most famous criminals. Newspapers sold out when they contained stories about Frank and Jesse James. Some of the public even admired the James gang. Their crimes were daring—and sometimes even fair-minded. For example,

This photo, taken in the 1870s, shows Jesse (left) and Frank James (right) and their mother. Frank was tried for murder and armed robbery but was found not guilty. He retired to his family's farm and died in 1915 at seventy-two years old.

they refused to rob men who had rough skin on their hands. They believed these men were hard workers and deserved to keep their money.

Lawmen were determined to take down the gang. Railroad companies were angry over having their employees harmed and their property stolen and destroyed. The Union Pacific Railroad hired the Pinkerton National Detective Agency to stop the James gang. In January 1875, the Pinkerton Agency raided Frank and Jesse's mother's house. They were convinced that Jesse and Frank were hiding there. They tossed a stick of dynamite through the window. The explosion injured Frank and Jesse's mother and killed their half brother. Worried about their family's safety, the James brothers took a three-year break from crime.

Back in Business

In 1879, Jesse James resumed his criminal career. Jesse's new crimes were far more brutal. He lost the admiration of the American public. Journalists who once supported him now demanded that he be stopped. In 1881, the police caught several gang members. A ten-thousand-dollar reward was offered for the capture of Jesse.

On April 3, 1882, two fellow gang members betrayed Jesse. Jesse had just finished eating breakfast with Bob and Charlie Ford. Jesse went into the living room and noticed that his favorite picture was dusty. Jesse put down his gun and stood on a chair to dust the picture. His back was to the Ford brothers. This was the moment for which they had been waiting. Bob aimed at Jesse and fired. Jesse tumbled off the chair and died instantly. The police took days to identify Jesse's body. They wanted to make sure that his death was not a hoax.

Butch Cassidy and the Sundance Kid
Butch Cassidy and the Sundance Kid were the last train and bank robbers of the Wild West. Cassidy was a fun-loving, easygoing bandit. He was born in Utah in 1866 as Robert LeRoy Parker. He became a cowboy in his teens and turned to crime when he began rustling cattle. Butch committed his first successful bank robbery in 1889. That year he stole thirty-one thousand dollars. Butch spent two years in jail from 1894 to 1896. Upon release, he went directly to the Hole-in-the-Wall, a hideout in the Colorado Mountains.

There Butch met the Sundance Kid, whose real name was Harry Longbaugh. Longbaugh

Many movies have been made about the lives of outlaws. In Butch Cassidy and the Sundance Kid, *actors Robert Redford (left) and Paul Newman (right) portrayed the outlaws.*

was born in Pennsylvania in 1867 and started stealing horses while still in his teens. He got thrown into the Sundance jail in Wyoming, where he earned his nickname. Once he met Butch Cassidy, the two decided to form a new gang. This gang was called the Wild Bunch.

Crimes by the Bunch

The Wild Bunch committed many robberies between 1896 and 1899. On June 2, 1899, the gang tried to rob a train at Wilcox,

Wyoming. When a guard refused to hand over the safe, Butch lit a stick of dynamite. He placed it next to the door. The guard, along with thirty thousand dollars in banknotes, was blown out of the train.

The Pinkerton National Detective Agency was hired to track the bandits. Four lawmen were killed in the bloody chase. By 1901, the Wild Bunch split up. But Butch and Sundance continued their crime spree. This time, though, they were outlaws on another continent. They spent two years robbing banks in South America. In 1908, Butch and Sundance were both killed during a shoot-out with soldiers in Bolivia.

·FRONTIER FACT·

Some people believe that the Sundance Kid had been shot several times and wounded by the soldiers in Bolivia. Rather than let his friend be caught alive, Butch Cassidy shot the Sundance Kid in the head.

CHAPTER 4

LIVING LEGENDS

Female Outlaws

Female outlaws also left a mark on the Wild West. They boldly went against the law to get what they wanted. One of the most famous female outlaws was Belle Starr. Starr started the outlaw life when she became involved with Cole Younger.

Younger was a member of Jesse James's gang. Later she married Sam Starr and their ranch became a hideout for outlaws. Her crimes included horse stealing and robbing a post office.

Pearl Hart is another well-known outlaw. She is known for being a part of the last stagecoach robbery. In 1899, she and a miner, Joe Boot, held up a stagecoach using guns. It was Hart's first robbery. She and Boot were caught and sentenced to prison. Hart escaped jail but was caught again.

Belle Starr was charged with many crimes and was known as the Bandit Queen. However, she was convicted for only one crime in her lifetime. The crime was taking two horses that did not belong to her.

35

The Mystery of Billy the Kid

Over one hundred years have passed since the death of Billy the Kid. Yet he continues to fascinate people. Billy the Kid has been the subject of many movies and books. Even scientists and historians continue to examine his life.

A fierce debate among historians continues over Billy the Kid's death. Did Billy really die in 1881? Some people believe his death was a hoax. Records say that Pat Garrett killed Billy in 1881. Officially, Billy is buried in Fort Sumner, New Mexico. However, in 1950, at the reported age of ninety-one, Brushy Bill Roberts from Texas claimed to be Billy the Kid. Then in 1993, Helen Airy wrote a book claiming that Arizonian John Miller was the real Kid.

To discover the truth, New Mexico officials want to dig up the remains from the graves of Billy the Kid, Roberts, and Miller. They also want to dig up the grave of Billy's mother, Catherine Antrim. Antrim is buried in Silver

This is a photograph of Bob Ford, one of the brothers responsible for killing Jesse James. On November 12, 2003, Ford's gun was sold for $350,000 in an auction.

City, New Mexico. They will remove and test DNA from all four skeletons. If the DNA of one of the men matches Catherine's, scientists would be able to identify which grave holds the real Billy the Kid.

In November 2003, the investigation came to a halt. The mayors of Fort Sumner and Silver City stopped the digging. The diggings and DNA tests are stalled for now. Without these tests, the mystery of Billy the Kid may never be solved.

Best of the West

As America expanded westward, life grew more difficult and dangerous. Many people moved to the West with dreams of striking gold or owning land. Cities grew faster than their sheriffs could handle. However, some people's dreams did not come true. Some struggling pioneers turned to lives as outlaws. Others felt it was their duty to protect those men and women who had come to the West to make a better life.

Though they were usually enemies, the lawmen and the outlaws of the Wild West had a lot in common. They were clever, fearless, and determined men and women. During the

After Jesse James was shot, his mother opened up his house as a museum and sold pebbles from his grave for twenty-five cents as souvenirs. Above is an illustration of Jesse James and his home.

late nineteenth century, the United States was going through growing pains. The new nation was changing by the day. In many ways, these outlaws and lawmen led the nation through these changing times.

OTHER FAMOUS FIGURES

Many lesser-known lawmen and outlaws from the Wild West have rich and interesting stories. Here are just a few:

Black Bart

BLACK BART was a lone stagecoach robber who dressed in white. Bart set up dummies in the woods to pose as hidden gang members. He also left poems he wrote in the empty money boxes after robbing a stagecoach.

Isom Dart

ISOM DART changed his name from Ned Huddleston to escape lawmen. Dart stole horses and cattle. When Dart was finally captured, he helped a sheriff who was hurt. The sheriff helped Dart at his trial and he was set free.

WILD BILL HICKOK was a lawman with a lightning quick draw. He was murdered in 1876 during a poker game. His cards, a pair of aces and a pair of eights, became known as the dead man's hand.

Wild Bill Hickok

ALLAN PINKERTON started the Pinkerton National Dectective Agency in 1850. In 1866 the agency caught the bandits responsible for stealing $700,000 from the Adams Express Company. Also, Pinkerton and his organization were responsible for foiling a plot to murder President Abraham Lincoln.

Allan Pinkerton

NEW WORDS

avenge (uh-**venj**) to take revenge or satisfaction

boomtown (**boom**-toun) a town that has sudden growth in business and population

confrontation (kuhn-**fruhn**-tay-shun) a meeting with someone in a threatening or accusing way

deputy (**dep**-yuh-tee) a person who helps or acts for someone else, as in a sheriff's deputy

DNA (**dee en ay**) the molecule that gives living things their special characteristics

folklore (**fohk**-lore) the stories, customs, and beliefs of ordinary people that are passed down to their children

frontier (fruhn-**tihr**) the far edge of a country, where few people live

hoax (**hoax**) a trick or a practical joke

marshal (**mar**-shul) an officer of a federal court who has duties similar to those of a sheriff

notorious (noh-**tor**-ee-uhss) to be well known for doing something bad

posses (poss-eez) groups of people gathered together by a sheriff to capture criminals

prospectors (pross-pekt-uhrs) people who explore an area for valuable metals or oil

racism (ray-siz-uhm) a belief that a particular race is superior to others

saloon (suh-loon) a bar where people can buy and drink alcoholic beverages

sawmill (saw-mil) a place where people use machines to saw logs into lumber

souvenir (soo-vuh-nihr) an object that you keep to remind you of a place, a person, or an event

tuberculosis (tu-bur-kyuh-loh-siss) a very contagious disease that affects the lungs

vigilante (vij-uh-lan-tee) an unauthorized citizen or group that fights crime and punishes criminals

FOR FURTHER READING

Epstein, Dwayne. *Lawmen of the Old West.* Farmington Hills, MI: Gale Group, 2004.

Glass, Andrew. *Bad Guys: True Stories of Legendary Gunslingers.* Madison, WI: Turtleback Books, 2000.

Murray, Stuart. *Wild West.* New York: Dorling Kindersley Publishing, Inc., 2001.

Stewart, Gail, and Yoshi Miyaki. *Where Lies Butch Cassidy?* Parsippany, NJ: Silver Burdett Press, 1992.

Yancey, Diane. *Desperadoes and Dynamite: Train Robbery in the United States.* Danbury, CT: Scholastic Library Publishing, 1991.

Organizations

The Earp Society
P.O. Box 944
Colton, CA 92324
(909) 877-6113 or
(909) 352-1278
www.earpsociety.com

The Old West Living History Foundation
2608 $\frac{1}{2}$ Central Ave.
Cody, Wyoming 82414
(307) 587-1872
www.oldwest.org

RESOURCES

Web Sites

America's Story
www.americaslibrary.gov/cgi-bin/page.cgi/jb
Learn more about United States history on
this site.

California History: The Gold Rush
www.californiahistory.net/index.htm
Click on the links of this site to learn more about
California's gold rush. Also check out the
time line for more on U.S. history.

Cyber Soup's: The Wild West
www.thewildwest.org
This Web site provides information on lawmen
and outlaws as well as cowboys, cowgirls, rodeos,
and much more.

A
avenge, 24

B
Billy the Kid, 5, 22–25, 36–38
boomtown, 17–18, 22

C
Cassidy, Butch, 31–33
Civil War, 17, 27
confrontation, 5

D
deputies, 24, 25
DNA, 37

E
Earp brothers, 19–21
Earp, Wyatt, 18–20, 22

G
Garrett, Pat, 5, 25, 36
gold rush, 6, 9–11

H
Holliday, Doc, 19–22

J
James gang, 28–29
James, Jesse, 27–31, 35

L
Lincoln County War, 24

M
Murrieta, Joaquín, 11–15

O
O.K. Corral, 21

INDEX

About the Author

Jessica Bard is a theater director and teacher in Los Angeles, California. She teaches acting and tutors children after school. When she was a teenager, she saw the movie *Young Guns*. She has been interested in the Wild West ever since. Now she enjoys making history fun for her students. She has written several stories and plays. This is her first published work.